SRL Publishing Ltd

Office 47396
PIO Box 6945
London, W1A 6US

Copyright © 2020 Ben Churchill

3 5 7 9 10 8 6 4

All rights reserved. No part of this publication may be reproduced or transmitted in any form or by any means, electronic, mechanical, photocopying or otherwise, without the prior permissions from the publisher.

All photos, design and recipes by Ben Churchill

Chef Ben Churchill hereby excludes all liability to the extent permitted by law for any error or omissions in this book and for any loss, damage or expense (whether direct or indirect) suffered by a third party relying on any information contained in this book.

All photos were taken by myself throughout my travels.

Locations include: Pickering, Cornwall, St. Albans, Yorkshire, Borehamwood, The Chilterns and the Forest of Dean.

ISBN 978-1-916337305

www.srlpublishing.co.uk
www.chefbenchurchill.com
www.facebook.com/thefoodillusionist
www.instagram.com/chefbenchurchill

Introduction 4
Equipment
    -basic essentials 9
    -specialist desirables 11
    -silicone moulds: 13
     an obsession
    - a note on stencils 16

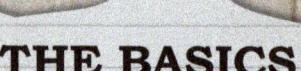

THE BASICS

cookie dough 20
-variations
basic sponge 21
chocolate brownie 22
meringue dust 23
chocolate ganache 23
tempering chocolate 24
carrot cake 25
swiss roll sponge 26
bavarois 27
flat mousse 29
custard 30
sugar syrup 31
mirror glaze 32

THE GARNISHES

soil 134
twigs 135
bark 135

hybrid sauces: from 136
sultana syrup to apple
pie puree

THE RECIPES

carrot cake 37
black forest 2.0 41
cold apple crumble 48
scotch bonnet cookie bites 55
egg custard pasta with chocolate truffle 59
beans on toast/ egg on toast 64
pannacotta scotch egg 70
stilton cheesecake 75
coffee and walnut cake 80
Sticks and stones 86
the washing up sponge 90
pizza cake 96
the chocolate brownie tree 101
chocolate orange yule log 108
the chocolate throne 114
the ashtray pannacotta 126

INTRODUCTION

First of all, this is not a cookbook. Not in the conventional sense of the word anyway. Sure, it has recipes in it, and methods and food. But it is more than that. Deeper than that. This book, I hope, will teach you how to think. How I think. I aim to capture and help you understand my ethos, my outlook, my thought process and my inspiration so you too can create your own food illusions.

Any book can teach you how to cook; which ingredients to buy, how much of each ingredient to use and how to prepare those ingredients. But you will never be left with something that is truly yours, that you dreamt up, that is truly original. This is absolutely fine, of course. The majority of most chefs' careers are spent just doing that, until you have your name above the door. But this book goes way beyond that. Anyone can learn my techniques and recipes, and all the ingredients can be bought from your local supermarket.

Cooking should be fun. Rules shouldn't be followed religiously. Cooking, like art, is about expression and story-telling. No one should be afraid to experiment and try new things in the kitchen.

One key thing that has given me this outlook is the fact that I'm self taught. I started as a pot wash in my local pub and climbed the ranks from there. But one thing I never bothered with is pastry. Sure I could bang out some decent tasting desserts, but I'd never explored further. Around 4 years ago I decided to change that and started teaching myself pastry. I soon got bored of the run of the mill stuff and wanted to explore further. I wondered if you could use food to trick, to amaze.

So I started to experiment, exploring. My first illusion was a chocolate lemon. Looking back it was so crude. I coated a lemon in yellow chocolate, broke it in half, filled it with ganache and stuck it back together. It was so amateur, but it woke me up. I was over the moon with how it turned out.

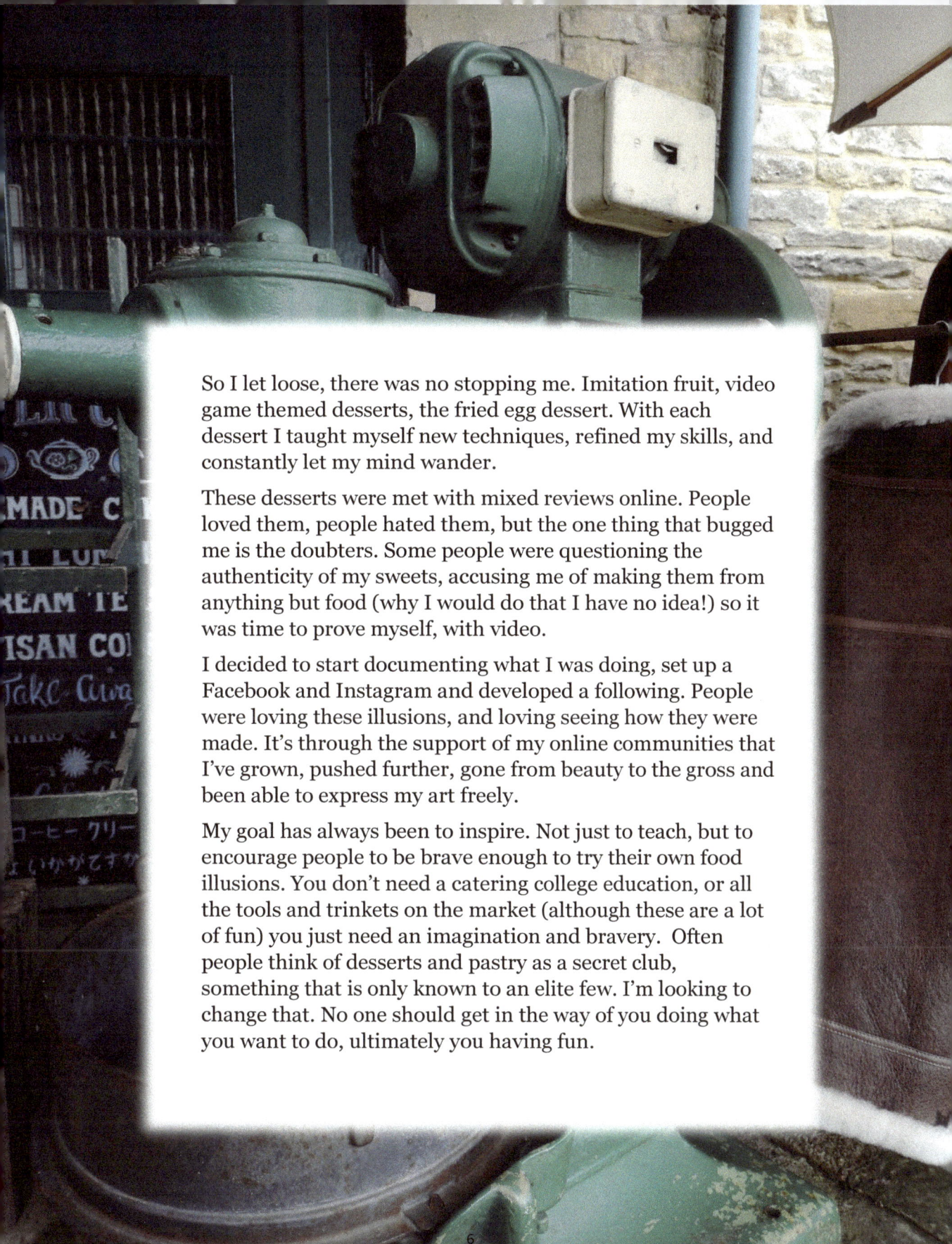

So I let loose, there was no stopping me. Imitation fruit, video game themed desserts, the fried egg dessert. With each dessert I taught myself new techniques, refined my skills, and constantly let my mind wander.

These desserts were met with mixed reviews online. People loved them, people hated them, but the one thing that bugged me is the doubters. Some people were questioning the authenticity of my sweets, accusing me of making them from anything but food (why I would do that I have no idea!) so it was time to prove myself, with video.

I decided to start documenting what I was doing, set up a Facebook and Instagram and developed a following. People were loving these illusions, and loving seeing how they were made. It's through the support of my online communities that I've grown, pushed further, gone from beauty to the gross and been able to express my art freely.

My goal has always been to inspire. Not just to teach, but to encourage people to be brave enough to try their own food illusions. You don't need a catering college education, or all the tools and trinkets on the market (although these are a lot of fun) you just need an imagination and bravery. Often people think of desserts and pastry as a secret club, something that is only known to an elite few. I'm looking to change that. No one should get in the way of you doing what you want to do, ultimately you having fun.

I like to think of cooking as problem solving. I always know what I want my outcome to be, but getting there is the adventure. There will be some trial and error, a bit of winging it, and a lot of improvisation, but that is half the fun. I know this outlook will make any pastry chef's blood run cold and beads of sweat to run down their neck, but desserts can be created in this way.

Let me give you an example...

I wanted to create an apple, this much I knew.

It was winter (Christmas had just left us) so my thoughts immediately turned to comfort food. And what better comfort food than apple crumble and custard? However, it was crisp outside, but sunny, so a steaming hot pudding was not what was needed. More an anticipated taste of spring, with memories of the bleakness we were leaving behind; a cold dessert with warm feelings.

For my filling I went for a bavarois. It has a smooth, creamy texture that is the perfect carrier for the warming flavours of apple and cinnamon that I was going for. A simple granola served as the crumble, albeit on the bottom, and an artful splatter of cold custard rounded the dish off perfectly. Finally, for my signature spin on it, a chocolate mirror glaze to coat the bavarois.

Hopefully, this sounds a simple enough process. It is; if you've got the mindset, imagination, and no limitations. Simply put, don't question whether it can be done or not, just ask yourself how.

"Don't question whether it can be done or not, just ask yourself how..."

EQUIPMENT

- BASIC ESSENTIALS
- SPECIALIST DESIRABLES
- SILICONE MOULDS: AN OBSESSION
- STENCILS: WHERE STREET ART MEETS FOOD

BASIC ESSENTIALS

Every domestic kitchen should (hopefully) have the basic equipment to be able to throw together food. We are going to start off assuming that you already have an oven, hob of some sort, fridge and freezer. Most of my recipes call for a smoothie blender and a food processor. Both can be picked up for relatively cheap. The smoothie blender is great for purees, fine blends, making small amounts of cake crumbs and chopping small amounts of ingredients so it will pay for itself, I promise you. You can use a food processor instead of a smoothie blender if needed, but you may not get the same refinement.

An electric whisk will also be necessary, and can save you a lot of elbow grease.

In terms of light equipment, we'll again assume that you have a sharp knife, mixing bowl, baking trays, chopping board, spoons, pastry brush, grater, rolling pin, a fine metal sieve, whisk, and some sort of counter space for working on. This is really all anyone needs to get started in a kitchen, but there are some cheap yet indispensable bits of kit that are a must if you want to take your desserts to the next level.

SCALES

One thing I will admit that'll have pastry chefs breathing a sigh of relief is that you'll need a decent set of electric scales to produce any pastry. Incorrectly weighed ingredients can mean the difference between a beautifully gooey brownie and a chocolate omelette. There is no need to break the bank with the latest, high precision set (as beautiful as they are); you should be able to get a decent working set for about a tenner. If you're anything like me they'll soon be covered in chocolate anyway!

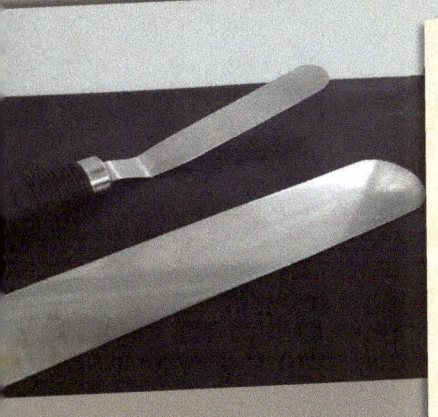

PALETTE KNIVES

In my opinion, palette knives are the second most important bit of equipment you can have. They have countless uses; from spreading melted chocolate, to lifting desserts into place, measuring, creating patterns, chopping, mixing, smoothing... Trust me, If you are ever in a jam, having one of these at your side will nearly always save the day. Two should do you; one about a foot long (preferably with an offset handle for spreading ingredients in a baking tray). The other one I can't do without is only the length of my middle finger but is perfect for the more intricate jobs. Its top selling point? Being able to fit in your back pocket. Trust me, you won't know you need it until you have it. Again these should only cost you a couple quid each.

SCALPEL/ CRAFT KNIFE

The single most important knife in my wrap is my craft knife. There are some jobs that are impossible with a chef's knife (or any other knife for that matter). Creating stencils: craft knife. Slicing sheets of frozen mousse: craft knife. Trimming chocolate work intricately: craft knife. For a couple of quid you can pick one up and change your dessert game forever. You'll need a cutting mat to go with it, but that shouldn't set you back much.

PLASTIC SPREADER

One of the biggest wastes of money on the market. Why buy something you can make yourself? You know the thing I mean; a small flat sheet of flexible plastic that you can use for stirring and spreading chocolate. A very handy bit of kit that you will find so useful alongside your palette knives. Here's how to get your hands on one for free (or the price of a tub of ice cream). Take the lid off a 2 litre tub of ice cream. Using your recently purchased craft knife (!) cut a rectangle approximately 10cm by 8 cm. On one edge, round two corners off to curves. And that's it. Done. Indispensable for chocolate work, and at a price that's right.

COCKTAIL STICKS

Cocktail sticks are something that you may never find a use for, but when you do you'll be glad you bought them. I find them perfect for dipping things into chocolate or glaze (especially spherical pieces) or creating holes to insert chocolate decorations. They're great for when you need to manoeuvre a part of your dessert but don't want to leave finger marks. And most importantly, they're so cheap that you can throw them away after each use!

PIPING BAGS

I highly recommend you buy disposable piping bags for your desserts for a number of reasons. You don't need nozzles for the end as you can cut holes for piping to your own requirements, however I recommend getting a set for when you want to pipe clean designs for garnishes etc. I use piping bags quite a lot in my food, so it saves you so much time and hassle if you don't have to worry about washing and drying each time. With a reusable bag you need to wash it out, then make sure it's bone dry before putting more chocolate in or you'll shock the chocolate. For my carrot cake you need the bags to mould the dessert in, and you'll need 6 of them, so it's actually more economic to buy disposable.

SPECIALIST DESIRABLES

ACETATE

Acetate is probably the only tool listed that will set you back a bit financially. Not horrendously (around £15 for 50 a4 sheets online) but it is a bit of an investment. If you wish to do superior looking chocolate work, specifically cylinders and wavy shapes, then you will need to splash out.

The other thing it is perfect for, is stencil making. If you want to create one off stencils then paper is more than fine, but there is something satisfying about building up a chocolate smattered folder full of acetate stencils, ready for use time and time again. But enough about stencilling, we'll get to that later...

BLOWTORCH

A blowtorch isn't absolutely essential, but there are recipes that call for it. You can stick 2 half spheres of frozen bavarois together just by pressing and smoothing the seal, but I promise you the end result will not be as polished as when you melt slightly with a blowtorch. Domestic ones can be picked up cheaply, and will do you just fine.

You'll find many uses for it outside of this book; toasting coconut, caramelising sugared fruit, even lighting the hob.

SQUEEZY BOTTLES

While not essential, they are such a cheap way of making your saucing neater and more professional looking. It's also a lot more organised and cleaner than pots and bowls of sauce all over the fridge!

A NOTE ON BAKING PARCHMENT...

Just a quick note on something that is so important. Baking parchment vs baking paper. Do not get caught out and buy baking paper, it's useless. I've never seen the point of it unless you want your food to stick in a horrible mess of disappointment. I can't stress enough the importance of buying parchment, not paper. I use it for lining baking trays, piping chocolate onto, even stencils at a push. It's a must.

DIGITAL THERMOMETER

An essential, really, if you are going to be making glazes, tempering chocolate and boiling sugar. You can pick them up cheaply and will definitely up your pastry game.

SILICONE MOULDS: AN OBSESSION

I can still remember my first time. My first one. The intrigue, anticipation, the excitement. Waiting for the right time. Waiting for it to finally be ready to take out the freezer, unmould and mirror glaze. The first mould I ever bought is one I still use today and probably still my favourite. When I started to open up my mind and explore what I can achieve in desserts, I quickly found that moulds would be a way to take it to the next level. That first mould, the 2 inch diameter half sphere silicone, is perfect.

I made my first apple dessert with that mould. An apple and cinnamon bavarois served with a rolled cinnamon tuille to resemble a cinnamon stick. It filled me with awe. How cool this dessert looked, with such a simple and cheap technique. So my mind started wandering, where next? What else is out there? What else can I do? So I ordered myself a couple more; the silicone muffin mould gave birth to the first plant pot dessert. A 1 inch half dome then gave me the idea for the scotch egg, meaning I could create a yolk inside a larger sphere of pannacotta "white". But this was only the beginning. I started discovering the novelty moulds available and things really took off. Star wars, Lego bricks, turntables, even Tetris block moulds, every type of mould imaginable.

Every trip into town with my wife and daughter would always manage to get steered towards my favourite hotspots. I'm not talking about cook shops, but discount department stores, home stores, the places that sell random bric a brac for the kitchen. I'd rummage through the piles of discounted stock until I found something, and suddenly my mind would start racing. What can I do with this one?

I have a permanent and ever growing shopping list in the back of my mind of moulds I need. I'll give you an example. For months I'd been searching for a way of making a Tetris mousse dessert. The first one I made was crude as all the pieces were hand cut from a big block of frozen mousse. I searched and searched but I just couldn't find what I needed, perfectly square shaped moulds. Around 8 months later I was just walking round a novelty gift shop and there it was. An ice cube tray. But not just any old ice cube tray, one that made perfectly square cubes of ice... or bavarois. I'd found it! And I knew just what to do with it.

It came to a point, however, when I realised that there are certain moulds you just won't be able to buy. Ever. A spray can nozzle for example, no one on earth makes these commercially. So where to get one?

The answer came in the form of food safe silicone putty. Relatively amateur, but also cheap and perfect for the beginner. Mix part one to part two, mould around object and leave to set. What could go wrong?

The result was better than I could ever imagine. Now the sky really was the limit. I made my spray can nozzle, but then so much more. the pannacotta egg, the first xenomorph egg, the pear.

I haven't really covered the use of moulds much in this book, apart from a couple of recipes where the plant pot and spheres are used, as I think unless you can get your hands on the particular mould, the recipe is useless. But the real reason, I think, is that I believe using moulds in your cooking is so personal, something that gets your mind and imagination really working. Only you can really work out what flavour you think BB8 from Star Wars should be, if you can find the mould, or what filling would go well in that dollar sign chocolate mould. Once you get the taste for creating something unique hopefully you'll get the bug too.

Just don't ask where my hotspots are.

STENCILS: WHERE STREET ART MEETS FOOD

16 year old me, when I look back, was a bit of a pretentious arsehole. I desperately wanted to be the next big modern artist. I was in awe of the 90's art movement. The shock factor, outrageousness, almost rock star-like behaviour of these artists. My work reflected this, or so I thought.

My other great artistic love was, and still is, graffiti. When I wasn't pissing off my tutors with shock pieces, I was doodling and refining my reaches, and pieces in my sketch book.

Years later, that love of graffiti has played a massive part in my work, in the form of stencil art. Nothing draws the attention and makes a plate talk like a chocolate stencilled face of the Joker, or paying homage to the man himself, a Banksy rat painting Merry Christmas over my mince pies.

There are plenty of places to purchase and download stencils, which is brilliant! Simply print out or order, cut out with a scalpel and start tagging them plates. You can use normal paper for one off stencils, but for repeated use you are going to need to invest in some acetate (washable and durable).

But what about custom stencils? What if you want a stencilled selfie of your face, or your logo, or as mentioned the Joker from Suicide Squad? Well here's my secret.

There are a number of apps available for your phone that convert any picture into a stencil. Once printed it will still need a keen eye and artistic hand to make into a stencil that works, but 95 percent of the work will be done for you. If creating with acetate, simply print out your stencil, tape on top of your acetate and then cut out firmly.

Now get tagging.

THE BASICS...

There are certain recipes which form the base of a lot of my desserts. I'm not going to include your usual cakes and desserts, only the ones that are relevant. Feel free to tweak them as needed, I certainly do! And never be afraid to alter and change a recipe. If you find this gets a better end product, brilliant!

NOTE

I measure all ingredients in grams (g), even fluids, unless stated otherwise. I find this to be a much more accurate method as there's no faffing about with a jug. It also means you can weigh all your ingredients into the same bowl, reducing washing up and meaning you don't lose any ingredient by it sticking to the side of jugs.

Please note that all my measurements, oven temperatures and currency references are coming from an British perspective. I apologise for the lack of conversions, but if needed you'll be able to easily convert to your chosen unit online or using one of the many apps available.

All oven temperatures are in degrees Celsius, represented by a C.

COOKIE DOUGH

Not actually used for making cookies, this is a brilliant way of using up leftover cake trimmings, stale cakes etc. While not exactly like cookie dough itself, it reminds me of it texturally and is so moreish. It's great as a layer in a cake, to mould into any shape either in a silicone mould or freehand, and can be frozen and mirror glazed without losing any of its qualities. It must be noted that this is a general ratio, and you may find that you need to add a bit more melted chocolate or syrup, depending on the cake crumb used.

INGREDIENTS
100g sponge cake
50g golden syrup

METHOD
Blitz the sponge in a food processor until finely crumbed, about 30 seconds on a high speed.
Mix the golden syrup in by hand until fully incorporated. At this stage, you can add any flavourings you choose. This can then be either moulded by hand or shaped in a silicone mould, and will set to a lovely texture in the fridge. Even better, it can be frozen and then glazed and will defrost without losing its texture or taste.

VARIATIONS

BROWNIE COOKIE DOUGH

INGREDIENTS

100g brownie
50g melted dark chocolate
25g golden syrup

METHOD

Blitz the brownie in a food processor to crumbs. This should take around 30 seconds.
Mix the crumbs with the syrup and melted chocolate and use exactly like quick cookie dough.

CHOCOLATE COOKIE DOUGH

To turn your basic cookie dough into a chocolate one without brownie, you can just add in some melted chocolate, a nice cheat to turn plain cake into a more indulgent one post bake. Follow the same method as the previous cookie dough ones.

INGREDIENTS

100g crumbed sponge
50g melted chocolate (white or dark, depends what the recipe calls for)
25g golden syrup

BASIC SPONGE CAKE

The most basic of cakes, but also one of the most vital, hence why it is included. The main thing I use this cake for is to make cookie dough.

Makes a 10 inch round cake tin half full when baked.

INGREDIENTS

250g self raising flour
5 medium eggs
250g butter (softened)
250g granulated sugar
1 teaspoon vanilla essence

METHOD

Preheat your oven to 170 degrees C (fan oven). Cream together the butter and sugar in your food processor until it starts to get light and fluffy. Add in the eggs and blitz until all mixed in. Finally, add your vanilla and flour and mix until a smooth cake batter is achieved. This can then be poured into your cake tin (with parchment on the bottom) and baked in the centre of the oven for around 15 minutes.

The trick to finding out if your cake is cooked is to insert a skewer or sharp knife into the centre and removing it slowly. If there is no cake batter on the knife it is cooked through. If there is some wet batter still on the knife, bake for a couple minutes more and check again. Once cooked, remove from the oven and cool. You can remove it from the tin after about 10 minutes and continue cooling further.

For a chocolate cake, replace 50 grams of flour with cocoa powder.

CHOCOLATE BROWNIES

This right here is a double whammy. Not only do you need my brownie recipe to make moulded desserts like the maple tree but it's also the best brownie recipe you will find!

Makes a 10 inch by 8 inch tray about 1 inch thick, which equates to 8 pieces plus off cuts from the edges (for making cookie dough, remember?)

INGREDIENTS

- 250g butter
- 250g dark chocolate (broken up pieces or even better, pellets)
- 125g plain flour
- 60g cocoa powder
- 5 large eggs
- 415g granulated sugar

METHOD

Preheat your fan oven to 165 degrees C. First, melt the butter slowly over a low heat. Once it's melted, whisk in the chocolate until it's all dissolved. Meanwhile, whisk the eggs with the sugar for around 3 minutes on high speed. The mix should turn pale and glossy. Pour your chocolate and butter over this and mix together until all blended. Finally, sieve the flour and cocoa into the mix and again, mix together till smooth.

Pour your brownie mixture into a 10 inch by 8 inch tin lined with parchment. Bake at 165 degrees C for around 25 minutes. Bear in mind that if you insert a skewer, it should come out slightly covered in brownie so the skewer test is not a good indicator of doneness in this case.

MERINGUE DUST

A great little garnish and in my opinion, better than icing sugar for dusting. This is not so much a recipe as a method. I'm not going to teach you how to make meringues, there are enough brilliant recipes out there...

METHOD

Take some meringues. You can use bought in or make your own, as long as they aren't burnt or oven marked in any way (we're looking for pure white here). Blitz them in your food processor and check every 30 seconds. Once you get the size you want, you'll know.

For garnishing, imagine the same size as granulated sugar. If you keep going however, you can achieve your very own icing sugar. Essential for wintertime dusting.

CHOCOLATE GANACHE

INGREDIENTS

100g double cream

200g good quality dark chocolate

METHOD

Warm the cream in a small saucepan until just starting to bubble. Meanwhile, place your chocolate in a heat proof bowl and as soon as those bubbles appear, pour the cream over the chocolate, whisking constantly until fully incorporated and thickened. For filling a tart, pour whilst still warm. If you plan to use to make truffles etc. Place in the fridge for approximately 1 hour before moulding.

A note on tempering chocolate

Tempering is basically a way of reworking chocolate to give it a better shine, finish and texture. You are essentially breaking down the structure of the chocolate and re-setting it. I won't go into the science here (even though it is fascinating) but I will give you a basic method to achieve this. It must be noted that different temperatures are needed for different types of chocolate, so I'll just explain dark chocolate here.

Always make sure you use a good quality chocolate in your work, and make sure that the chocolate is broken up into even sized pieces when you melt it.

For this I've used 200g of dark chocolate. This is just to give you the ratios.

Place a small saucepan with an inch of water in on the hob on a medium heat. Take 150 g of the chocolate and place in a metal or glass bowl. Place this bowl on top of the saucepan. The bowl must be larger than the pan and the water must not touch the bowl. You've just made a bain marie!

Heat slowly, whisking constantly, and take off the heat as soon as the chocolate reaches 55 degrees C. Remove 50g of this melted chocolate to another container and put to one side.

Next take the remaining 50g of unmelted chocolate and add it into the 100g of melted (try and keep up!) whisking constantly until all melted together. What you are trying to do is bring the temperature of the chocolate down. Place this bowl in a cool part of the kitchen and whisk every 5 minutes, probing each time until the chocolate reaches 28 degrees C. You must make sure it has been whisked thoroughly so all the chocolate is the same temperature.

Finally, add your remaining 50g of melted chocolate, again whisking well. This should raise the temperature just slightly to 30-32 degrees C. Your chocolate can now be piped, poured into a mould, or spread onto a silicone sheet, whatever you are going to use it for. Set in the fridge for that satisfying snap!

CARROT CAKE

A brilliant stand-alone recipe, but essential for the carrot cake 2.0

Makes an 8 inch round cake of a good thickness

INGREDIENTS

300g self raising flour

4 large eggs

320g vegetable oil

400g brown sugar

120g ground up walnuts (blitz in your smoothie blender)

350g grated carrot (grate by hand, or you won't get the best texture)

2 heaped teaspoons ground cinnamon

METHOD

This one is easy. Preheat your fan oven to 165 degrees c. Then, simply chuck all the ingredients except the carrot into your food processor and blitz until a smooth batter is achieved. Mix in the grated carrot by hand at the end, then pour into your lined baking tin and bake for 40 minutes.

Note that it should still be moist inside, so sticking a skewer into the middle won't give a great indication of doneness.

SWISS ROLL SPONGE

Good for using as a layer in a cake, given its lightness and flexibility, or for a cylindrical shaped cake with a filling such as the chocolate orange log

Enough to make a layer 10 inch by 8 inch.

INGREDIENTS

4 large eggs, separated
100g granulated sugar
20g cocoa powder
Dash of vanilla flavouring

METHOD

Preheat your fan oven to 165 degrees c. Whisk the yolks with the sugar until they turn pale and puff up a bit. Whisk in the cocoa powder and vanilla until fully combined.

In a separate bowl, whisk the egg whites until stiff (do not over whisk or they will curdle).

Fold the two together slowly until fully mixed, but still fluffy.

Spread evenly into a parchment lined tin and bake for 6 minutes.

If you are going to use this for rolling (like a swiss roll), immediately cover with a damp tea towel as soon as you remove from the oven. This will help keep it mouldable but best to use as soon as cool.

BASIC BAVAROIS

Here is a classic, basic bavarois recipe. It can be used as is and is great for making moulded desserts, or you can experiment and add cooked fruit puree in to alter the flavour and texture. A great one to experiment with!

INGREDIENTS

110g double cream
250g milk
50g granulated sugar
2 eggs separated
10g gelatine (3 sheets)
1 teaspoon vanilla extract

METHOD

Whisk the yolks and sugar together at high speed for around 3 minutes (the mixture should turn quite pale).

Meanwhile, heat the milk and vanilla slowly but do not boil!

Take the milk off the heat and pour slowly onto your egg yolk mix, whisking constantly.

Return this mixture to your pan and again heat slowly, whisking constantly. Be careful as it will suddenly start thickening after a couple of minutes. You are looking for the consistency of a good custard; not too thick but can coat the back of a spoon. Beat in the soaked and drained gelatine, then set this custard aside to cool for about an hour, covered with cling film to avoid a skin forming.

After an hour, whisk your double cream until nice and thick, but be careful not to over whisk. Fold the cooled custard into the cream carefully until fully blended.

Next whisk your remaining egg whites into stiff peaks, then fold into the custard and cream mix.

The mix is now ready to be set. It can be piped into moulds, frozen then mirror glazed, or used from chilled to complement a dessert.

To create different flavours, fruit for example, I simply leave the double cream out and replace with the same quantity of fruit puree.

FLAT MOUSSE

This is something I'm still trying to find a name for. It's a recipe I came up with as a simpler way of making a bavarois style mousse. It's got a slightly smoother texture yet not as much firmness as a bavarois, but is gorgeous in it's own right. For now, I'm going to call it a flat mousse...

Makes enough to fill fourteen 2 inch diameter half sphere moulds

INGREDIENTS

250g double cream
200g white chocolate
10g gelatine (3 sheets)
160g milk

METHOD

Start off by soaking your gelatine in cold water for 10 minutes. Heat the cream and milk together slowly but do not reach boiling point. You want it to just start giving off steam. Whisk in the soaked and drained gelatine until dissolved.

Pour this mix over the chocolate and whisk until fully melted. This mix can now be used in a mould. Simply pour into your silicone moulds, freeze overnight, and they're ready to mirror glaze. Will be ready to eat after an hour in the fridge.

The milk can be substituted for the same weight of fruit puree, or you can add in spices such as cinnamon etc.

This recipe and method is different to the flat mousse used in my chocolate log but the outcome will be very similar. Either method can be used depending on the desired outcome.

CUSTARD

Nothing outstanding or revolutionary to this custard, but you'll need it for the cold apple crumble. Also, it's a solid recipe for when you need custard anyway.

INGREDIENTS

75g double cream
200g semi skimmed milk
1 large egg yolk
50g granulated sugar
1 teaspoon vanilla extract
8g cornflour

METHOD

Heat the milk, cream and vanilla extract slowly on a gentle heat. Meanwhile, whisk together the yolks, cornflour and sugar for around 2 minutes with an electric whisk. Slowly pour the hot liquid onto the egg mix and whisk to bring together. Pour the whole mix back into the saucepan and heat slowly, stirring constantly. Pay particular attention to the sides and bottom of the pan, as this is where the custard can catch and burn if you're not careful. You have to be vigilant as after a couple of minutes of no progress, it'll suddenly start to thicken quite rapidly. Keep stirring over the heat until you achieve the thickness you would like. As a guide, when it is thick enough to coat the back of a spoon it's ready. Can be served hot, or chilled for a cold dessert.

SUGAR SYRUP

INGREDIENTS

200g granulated sugar

200g water

Ridiculously easy to make, but needed a few times in my recipes so I thought it best to include it.

METHOD

Simply add both the sugar and water to a saucepan and heat slowly whilst whisking. Once the sugar has dissolved, remove from the heat and cool. Stored covered in the fridge, your syrup will last for a couple of weeks.

MIRROR GLAZE

So here it is. My secret weapon. The one recipe I am constantly asked for, and one of the few recipes I won't give out. I've shared this recipe with a grand total of 3 people in my lifetime, until now.

Every pastry chef who uses mirror glaze will have their own recipe; one they've tweaked and refined over and over again. Mine has got to a point where it is so simple, with not too many ingredients and a straight forward technique.

Glazing is something that you will need to practice, and perfection can only come from doing again and again. You'll get a feel for when the glaze is the right consistency, if you've used enough colour, if the temperature is just right.

Glaze colour is vital. Ensuring you have a strong enough hue is the key to a rich, shiny mirror glaze. Use too little and it'll either have a transparency or be pale. The best way of avoiding this is to use a professional product. If you use more of a weaker colouring it will simply make your glaze gloopy. Personally I use "Colour Splash" which is cheap, available in a huge range of colours and available to buy in most hobby and cooking shops.

Gels are far superior to liquids or even powders in my opinion as they are more concentrated than liquids and give a more even distribution when mixing in than powders.

The most important thing to remember is always have more than enough food colouring than what you need. There is nothing more disappointing, and I speak from experience here, than not having enough colouring for the task at hand. What was meant to be a deep, shiny black bavarois turned into a pale grey let-down. Be prepared!

INGREDIENTS

130g double cream
80g semi skimmed milk
30g golden syrup
200g white chocolate (broken up or chips)
4 sheets of gelatine
30g olive oil
food colouring gel

This recipe will give you enough to comfortably glaze six to eight small desserts. Any leftover can be kept in the fridge for up to a week and simply reheated for use again.

YOU'LL NEED AN ELECTRONIC THERMOMETER FOR ANY GLAZE RECIPE!

METHOD

This needs to be started around 2 hours before it is needed as the most crucial aspect for glazing is temperature. Start off by soaking your gelatine in cold water for 10 minutes until softened. While it is soaking, combine the double cream, milk and golden syrup in a saucepan. Heat slowly, stirring constantly until the syrup is fully melted. Remove the gelatine from the cold water and squeeze out any excess. Add the gelatine to the saucepan and keep on the heat, stirring always. As soon as it starts to boil, remove from the heat and pour onto your white chocolate, which should be waiting in a heatproof bowl. Whisk until the chocolate is completely melted, then whisk in the olive oil (this will help with the consistency and shine). Finally, whisk in your colour of choice. Pass your glaze through a fine mesh sieve into a clean bowl or container and put to one side. It is vital at this stage to check you have the colour right. The best way of doing this is to take some glaze on a spoon and pour back into the container. If the poured mix is not as bright as wanted, whisk in some more colouring.

Now, here is the crucial bit. Put your glaze somewhere cool in the kitchen, but not in the fridge. You need to cover your glaze container with clingfilm, to avoid a skin forming, but stir every 10 minutes to keep its fluidity. After around an hour, check the temperature with your electronic probe. The glaze is ready to use at 31 degrees C. Any cooler, it won't give an even coat and will turn gloopy. Any hotter and it won't give a thick enough coating and the bavarois will show through. Don't worry if it cools down too much, simply give it about 10 seconds in the microwave, pass through a sieve and try again.

In my experience, it takes between an hour and a half and 2 hours to come to temperature. When you hit 31 degrees C, give it a final sieve and you're ready to glaze...

USING MIRROR GLAZE

So you've got your mirror glaze. It's at the right temperature. You've got whatever it is that you want to glaze ready and frozen. But what now? How do you actually go about glazing?

There are two methods. The first is to dip something into your glaze. For this you need to make sure that the glaze is in a narrow container so your frozen dessert will be fully submerged. Simply insert a skewer or cocktail stick into the bavarois (or whatever you are using) and dunk it in and out of the glaze. Count 4 seconds as you do it; 2 seconds going in, 2 seconds coming out. If you feel that it needs a thicker layer of glaze, repeat immediately with the same method. Leave suspended above the pot of glaze for around 6-8 seconds to drain off any excess, then place carefully onto baking parchment. It is vital that you put onto parchment and not just onto a plate or tray as you will need to lift it off again once set.

Leave in the fridge for around 1 hour so the glaze can set and the dessert itself can defrost. Then, simply lift off the parchment with the use of a spatula and the cocktail stick, place on your plate, and carefully slide the spatula out from underneath, while putting pressure on the cocktail stick. Remove the stick and you're good to go!

The second method is the pour. This is better suited for desserts that are too big to dip into a pot of glaze, such as mirror glazed mousse cakes (a subject not covered in this book, but well worth looking into). You make and cool your glaze exactly as before, but this time you need to take your frozen dessert out of the freezer and sit atop a cup on top of a tray. The cup is so the glaze can drip off freely, leaving you a nice clean edge and the tray is to catch all the glaze that will drip off. This can either be saved for another use or discarded. Either way, the tray saves a lot of mess!

Once you have your dessert positioned on top of the cup, give your glaze a final stir and pour slowly onto the very top of your cake, from a height of about 15cm. The idea is to keep pouring until the glaze has completely covered your dessert with a nice even coating. You will need to pour in small circles to ensure even coverage. Once you are happy, take a small spatula or knife and run it round the bottom rim of the dessert, to remove most of the drips. Transfer the whole tray carefully to the fridge and leave for at least 1 hour, depending on the size of the dessert, to defrost.

The simplest way to finish a glazed cake is to take some chocolate or cake crumbs and press around the bottom of the dessert to tidy up any drips that have remained. Carefully lift off of the cup it is resting on and serve!

THE RECIPES

CARROT CAKE

SERVES 6

This recipe needs to be started about four and a half hours before serving, assuming your carrot cake is already made and cooled.

INGREDIENTS

for the carrot:
  510g of carrot cake (page 25)

for the glaze:
  130g double cream
  30g golden syrup
  200g white chocolate broken up into pieces
  80g semi skimmed milk
  4 sheets of gelatine
  20g olive oil
  orange gel food colouring

for the soil:
  180g blitzed brownie soil (page 134)

for the chocolate pots:
  300g dark chocolate
  20g cocoa powder

to garnish:
  12 cookie dough stones around one inch diameter (page 86)
  18 one inch long mint stalks each with 3 or so leaves on
  30g granulated sugar

ADDITIONAL EQUIPMENT...

wooden skewers
food processor
6 disposable piping bags
string
small saucepan
6 silicone plant pot moulds
hand whisk
container 3" across by 5" tall
dry pastry brush
electronic thermometer

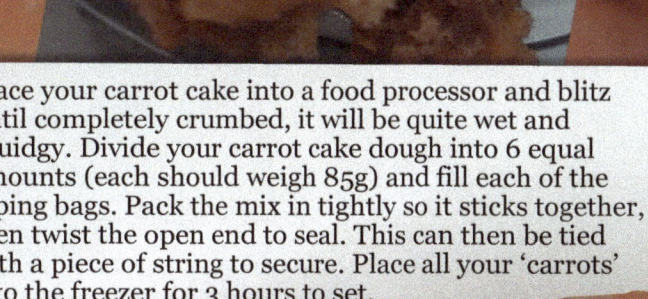

Place your carrot cake into a food processor and blitz until completely crumbed, it will be quite wet and squidgy. Divide your carrot cake dough into 6 equal amounts (each should weigh 85g) and fill each of the piping bags. Pack the mix in tightly so it sticks together, then twist the open end to seal. This can then be tied with a piece of string to secure. Place all your 'carrots' into the freezer for 3 hours to set.

Meanwhile, you can be making your garnishes. To make the carrot stalks, put the 30g of granulated sugar in a small saucepan with around 100g water. Heat slowly until the sugar has melted then add the 18 mint leaves with stalks. Bring to the boil then remove from the heat. Leave to cool for 30 minutes before removing the leaves and stalks from the water and patting dry between kitchen roll. Place these in the fridge for later.

To make the plant pots, first melt your chocolate. Pour 1/6 of it into one of your silicone pot moulds. Rotate the pot until the inside is completely coated then turn upside down over your bowl of melted chocolate to remove the excess (it may need a little shake). Tap the base of the pot mould onto the table to smooth out the coating. Run your finger round the rim to clean up the edge. Repeat for the other five moulds then place these in the fridge to set.

Now is a good time to prepare your cookie dough stones if you haven't already, and blitz your brownie for soil.

When your carrots have been in the freezer for one hour, you need to make your glaze. Soak your gelatine covered in cold water for 10 minutes to soften up. Place the double cream, milk, and golden syrup in a small saucepan and heat slowly. When bubbles start appearing around the edge, whisk in the gelatine, drained and squeezed of any excess water. Take off the heat and whisk in the oil. Put your white chocolate into a mixing bowl and pour the hot cream mix over it. Whisk well by hand for around 1 minute, until the chocolate is all melted and the mix is smooth. Still mixing, add your food colouring drop by drop until you achieve a "carrot orange" colour. Leave to one side covered for an hour and a half to two hours to cool down to 31 degrees c. Make sure you stir it every 10 minutes or so.

When your glaze has reached temperature, give it a good final stir and pour carefully into a short round container, around 3" across by 5" deep.
Remove your 'carrots' from the freezer and carefully cut off the piping bag from each. Smooth the rounded end of each with the palm of your hand to remove any ridges. Insert a skewer into the rounded end and, one by one, dip the 'carrots' into the glaze and remove slowly. Let any excess glaze drip off and carefully lay onto a plate with a piece of parchment on. Place them in the fridge to set for 45 minutes.

TO ASSEMBLE:

First, unmould your plant pots. Dust each with cocoa then brush off any excess. Less is more here.

Fill a chocolate pot with 30g of the brownie crumb and stand it on it's plate. Push it over, allowing the soil to spill as it does. Next pick up a "carrot" by the skewer. You may need to use a sharp knife to cleanly cut off the excess glaze and free from the parchment. Place this just in front of the pot, on the soil. Next put a couple of cookie dough stones alongside.

Lastly, carefully twist out the skewer, and replace with three of the poached mint stalks. Repeat for the rest of the carrot cakes.

May be served with pouring cream, if you like.

BLACKFOREST 2.0

SERVES 6 — You will need to start this recipe the day before serving as the cherry truffle needs to be frozen overnight.

ADDITIONAL EQUIPMENT...

2" diameter silicone half sphere moulds (you can buy these in a sheet of 15)
10" x 8" baking tray
fine sieve
cookie tray
small saucepan
spatula
electric or hand whisk
baking parchment
clingfilm
electronic thermometer
blowtorch

INGREDIENTS

for the sponge:
  200g butter melted
  4 medium eggs
  200g granulated sugar
  200g self raising flour
  50g cocoa powder
  1tsp vanilla extract

for the cherry truffle:
  200g tinned black cherries, drained weight (reserve the juice)
  400g dark chocolate pellets or broken up

for the glaze:
  200 g dark chocolate (at least 70% cocoa content) broken up into small pieces
  130 g double cream
  30 g olive oil
  120 g milk
  30 g golden syrup
  4 sheets gelatine
  good quality black and red food colouring gel

for the garnish:
  60g dark chocolate
  150g double cream
  50g icing sugar
  1 teaspoon vanilla extract

NOTE

This will make too much glaze but it won't work with a smaller amount. The leftover glaze can be kept in the fridge for a week and reused, or used in a chocolate sauce.

DAY ONE...

The truffle will need to be made a day ahead. Put the cherries into your smoothie blender and whizz for one minute or so until pureed. You may need to add a tablespoon of the juice from the tin to help the puree along. force the mix through a fine sieve to achieve a smooth puree. Weigh this puree and make up to 200g with the reserved juice from the tin. Transfer to a small saucepan and warm slowly. As the mixture starts to boil remove from the heat and whisk in the dark chocolate until fully melted. Pour this mix into twelve of the 2" half sphere moulds (that have been placed on a flat tray) and smooth off the top with a spatula. Freeze overnight.

The sponge will also need to be made today, allowing it time to cool and meaning you can prepare the rest of the dessert at your own pace tomorrow. Preheat your oven to 165 degrees C. Then, simply put all the cake ingredients into your mixing bowl and mix, either by hand or electric whisk, until you achieve a smooth batter with no lumps. Pour this cake mix into a 10" by 8" baking tray lined with parchment and bake for 24 minutes, until cooked through. Remove from the oven and leave to cool for 10 minutes, then flip onto a parchment lined cookie tray. Remove the baking tin and place on top to flatten the sponge as it cools. Once cool, wrap the sponge in clingfilm for tomorrow.

DAY TWO...

The next day, you'll need to prepare your glaze around two hours and 15 minutes before serving as it needs to cool down, and then needs to set. First soak your gelatine in cold water so it is completely covered. Take a small saucepan and heat your cream, milk and syrup until just boiling. Remove from the heat and pour into a bowl containing your dark chocolate. Whisk until melted then whisk in the oil and drained, squeezed gelatine. Finally whisk in enough black colouring to darken to an almost black colour, then some red to give it a red sheen when stirred. Pass through a fine sieve and then transfer to a plastic tub, around 3 inches across. Cover this with cling film and leave in a cool part of the kitchen. Make sure you stir every 15 minutes while it cools to 31 degrees C. This should take around one to one and a half hours.

While the glaze is cooling prepare your garnishes. In a clean bowl whisk your cream, adding the icing sugar a teaspoon at a time. you are looking for stiff peaks without over whisking. I find it best to bring to medium peaks with and electric whisk, then add your vanilla and slowly whisk in by hand. You will notice it thicken with each rotation so can judge a lot better. cover the bowl with cling film and refrigerate until needed.

Next take your sponge and trim one centimetre off each edge and trim the top flat if it has risen during cooking. Cut it once down the middle lengthways then three times widthways to create eight equal rectangles. Put six to one side and blitz the other two pieces in your food processor to crumbs. You will need 100g of these crumbs for serving, the rest can be used in another dish as either soil or cookie dough.

Next melt your chocolate, either in the microwave or in a bain marie but don't overheat. Transfer to a piping bag and tie the open end. Line a baking tray with parchment. Cut a 1mm hole off the end of the bag and pipe your cherry stalks. I always pipe more than needed just in case. Cut the hole another millimetre bigger then pipe some twigs, about 3-5 inches long, of different shapes. You need one stalk and two twigs per serving. When you are happy you have enough, put the tray in the fridge to set.

Now you can start to bring the whole thing together. When your glaze has cooled to 31 degrees C it is ready to use. If still too warm, leave a bit longer. If the temperature has dropped too far, don't panic! Simply place your tub of glaze in a shallow bowl of hot water and stir. Keep doing until the temperature comes back up. If it has dropped too far you may need to microwave in short bursts. If the glaze seems lumpy at this stage, pass through a sieve until smooth.

Take your silicone mould out the freezer and unmould half of the frozen half spheres. Working quickly, pass a blowtorch over the still moulded ones for half a second each and press a half sphere truffle on top. You should end up with six full sphere truffles.

Get your six plates ready, it's going to get a bit frantic. Place a piece of chocolate sponge on each one, slightly off centre. Next place a chocolate cherry truffle on top of each sponge. Pour some glaze on each one so it smoothly covers the whole truffle and runs a bit onto the sponge and plate. Place your plates into the fridge to set the glaze for around half an hour.

Now to finish and serve your plates. Start by taking a heaped tablespoon of the cake crumb and putting next to the sponge. Create a quenelle of the whipped cream (there's no harm in it being a dollop!) and carefully position on top of the crumb. Place 2 twigs on the plate, then finally make a small hole in the top of the glazed truffle and stick a chocolate stalk in the top.

COLD APPLE CRUMBLE

SERVES 5 — This recipe will need to be started a day in advance as the bavarois needs to be frozen overnight.

ADDITIONAL EQUIPMENT...

- small saucepan
- microwaveable container
- fine sieve
- electric whisk
- electronic thermometer
- mixing bowl
- 1" diameter silicone half sphere moulds (to make ten half spheres)
- Silikomart professional apple mould (makes 5)
- flat tray that fits in the fridge
- plastic tub to hold your mirror glaze
- baking parchment
- piping bags
- cocktail sticks
- smoothie blender

INGREDIENTS

for the vanilla bavarois:
- 565g semi skimmed milk
- 280g double cream
- 3 sheets of gelatine (12 g)
- 100g granulated sugar
- 4 egg yolks
- vanilla extract

for the apple filling:
- 200g peeled and cored apple
- 50g brown sugar
- 1 teaspoon cinnamon powder

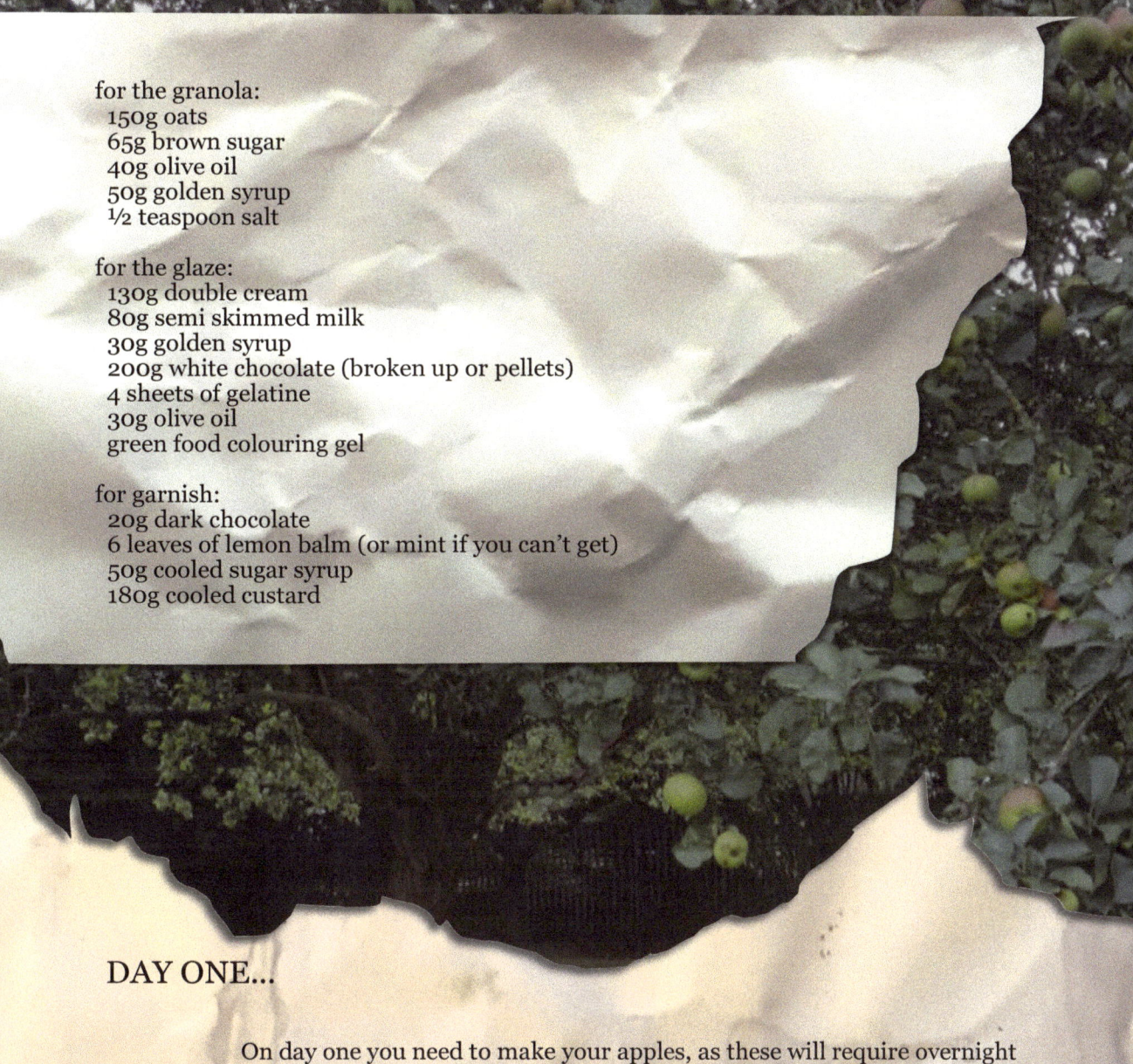

for the granola:
  150g oats
  65g brown sugar
  40g olive oil
  50g golden syrup
  ½ teaspoon salt

for the glaze:
  130g double cream
  80g semi skimmed milk
  30g golden syrup
  200g white chocolate (broken up or pellets)
  4 sheets of gelatine
  30g olive oil
  green food colouring gel

for garnish:
  20g dark chocolate
  6 leaves of lemon balm (or mint if you can't get)
  50g cooled sugar syrup
  180g cooled custard

DAY ONE...

On day one you need to make your apples, as these will require overnight freezing. Start off by making your apple filling by cutting your apple into 5mm dice. Put this into a microwaveable container with the sugar, Cinnamon and a tablespoon of water. Cover with clingfilm and microwave for around 4 minutes. Check that the apple has softened, but not to a mush (if needed, nuke for a minute or two more). Divide the mix between your one inch half sphere moulds, giving you ten in total. Put these in the freezer for around 5 hours to freeze.

About an hour before your apple filling is ready, you can prepare the bavarois mix. Start by whisking together the egg yolks and sugar until pale (around four minutes with an electric whisk). Meanwhile, soak your gelatine in cold water to soften. Next heat the milk and vanilla essence (the amount of vanilla you use will depend on the quality of your product. You want it to have the flavour without being too overpowering).

When just below boiling, remove from the heat and whisk in the egg yolk mix. Return the pan to the heat and whisk. Constantly. The mixture is going to go from nothing to thick very quickly so you can't take your eyes off it. When you get it to the consistency of thick double cream, remove from the heat and whisk in the gelatine which has been drained and squeezed of all excess water. Set aside covered for an hour to cool down.

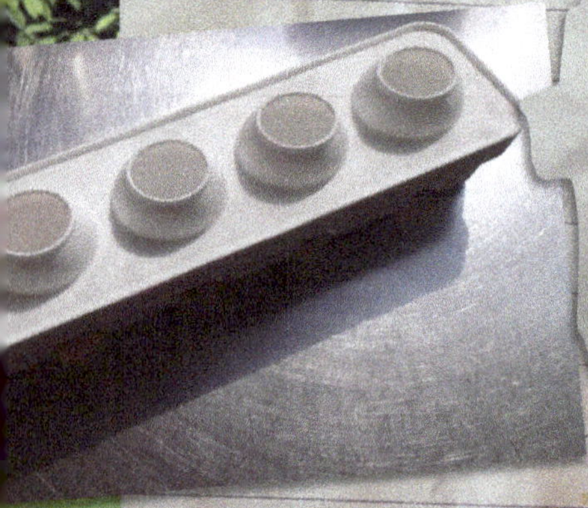

After an hour, whisk the cream till whipped and fold into the cooled mixture carefully until smooth.
Pass through a fine sieve into a jug for pouring.

Take your apple mould and fill each about 50 percent with the bavarois. Take your apple half spheres out the freezer and put together in pairs to make five balls. Place one each into the mould, ensuring it is central. Finally top each up with the remaining bavarois and smooth over.

Freeze overnight.

Next comes the granola, as you want it to be nice and cool and rested before eating. Simply take all your ingredients and mix by hand until everything is mixed together nicely and consistently. Spread it evenly on an oven try and bake at 165 degrees c . It'll need about 12 minutes but you must check it every 5 and give it a good stir to avoid burning. Once cooked (think the colour of flapjack) remove from the oven and leave to cool as is overnight.

If you are making your custard for this recipe (no one will judge you if you use tinned) now is a good time to do so, so you can chill it for serving on tomorrow's dessert.

The final thing to do today is the sugar glazed leaves. If you can get your hands on lemon balm it is a must for this dessert, but mint makes a good substitute, however the flavour marriage won't be quite the same. Simply submerge 6 leaves of the right size and shape in your sugar syrup, pull out by the stalk and wipe off any excess, but still leave a good coating. Place on a small sheet of parchment and leave somewhere dry overnight like the kitchen side.

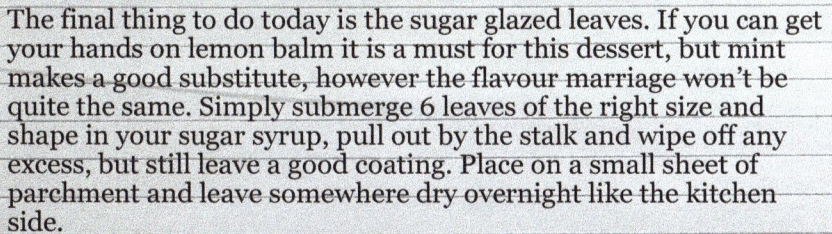

DAY 2...

You need to start this stage four hours before you intend to serve.

Today will be an easier day, and a more exciting one; the day it all comes together. The first thing you need to do is make the glaze as this takes time to cool down. First soak your gelatine as before, in cold water. Then in a small saucepan combine your double cream, milk and golden syrup. Heat slowly, stirring constantly and, when bubbles start to form on the edges whisk in your drained and squeezed gelatine until fully combined. Remove the pan from the heat and pour the contents into a large bowl that contains your white chocolate, whisking furiously to completely melt. Add your olive oil and, still whisking, add your food colouring bit by bit. Be very careful not to add too much at first, as you can't lighten the colour!

Keep adding until you achieve the shade of green you are after. Pour your glaze through a fine sieve into your plastic container and leave on the counter to chill covered in clingfilm. Make sure you stir it every 10 minutes to stop a skin forming It is ready to be used at around 31 degrees C. Any warmer and it won't glaze properly, any cooler and it won't give a smooth coating. This should take between one and a half and two hours.

The trick is to leave covered in cling film and give it a stir every 10 minutes or so. If it becomes too cold and thick, submerge the mug in a pot of hot water and stir until you reach 31 degrees and the glaze turns liquid again.

While the glaze is coming down to temperature, you can make your chocolate stalks. Melt your chocolate until it's just melted (microwave is probably best here, in 10 seconds bursts and stirring each time). I'd suggest using more chocolate than stated, so you've got more to work with. Put the melted chocolate in a disposable piping bag and cut the end off, making a 2mm hole. Pipe one inch stalk shapes onto baking parchment, with a lump at one end. It doesn't matter if the other end is scruffy, it'll be stuck into the apple! Pipe a few extra just in case, and set in the fridge until needed.

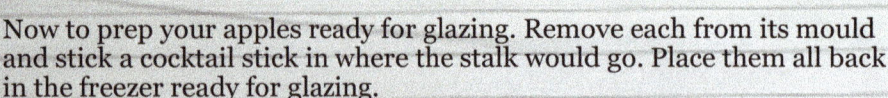

Now to prep your apples ready for glazing. Remove each from its mould and stick a cocktail stick in where the stalk would go. Place them all back in the freezer ready for glazing.

Time to mirror glaze. Have a tray ready with a sheet of parchment on that will fit in your fridge.

Take your glaze (check the temperature is correct) and give it a final stir, checking you have no lumps. One by one submerge your bavarois apples in the glaze and pull out, holding the cocktail stick. Hover over the cup of glaze for around 10 seconds to allow the excess to run off and then place carefully onto the parchment. Place the tray in the fridge for an hour to set.

TO ASSEMBLE...

Take a good spoonful of your cold custard and pour on your plate in the centre. Using the back of the spoon, hit into the custard gently to create a splat on the plate. Next, pile a couple of spoonful's of your granola into the centre of the plate.

With the aid of the cocktail stick and a small spatula, lift one of your apples off the parchment (it doesn't matter if the bottom is messy, it will be covered) and press onto the granola. Push the granola around a bit to cover any messy glazing. Remove the cocktail stick and insert a chocolate stalk. Finally, take a sugar glazed leaf of lemon balm and place with the stalk. Leave the dish out for 30 minutes before serving. Goes well with sultana syrup or apple pie puree, if you like.

SCOTCH BONNET COOKIE BITES

MAKES 6

This is a relatively quick and easy recipe. It should take 2 and a half to 3 hours to make.

INGREDIENTS

for the cookie dough:
200g vanilla sponge crumbs
50g golden syrup
20g sugar
50g dark chocolate
one fresh scotch bonnet
20g olive oil
6 mint stalks 1 inch long

for the glaze:
65g double cream
15g golden syrup
100g white chocolate (broken into small, even pieces)
2 sheets gelatine
10g olive oil
40g semi skimmed milk
red food colouring gel
1 large potato cut in half

ADDITIONAL EQUIPMENT...

food processor
smoothie blender
mixing bowl
small container for your glaze to go in
fine sieve
baking parchment
small saucepan
fondant icing modelling tool
electronic thermometer
6 cocktail sticks

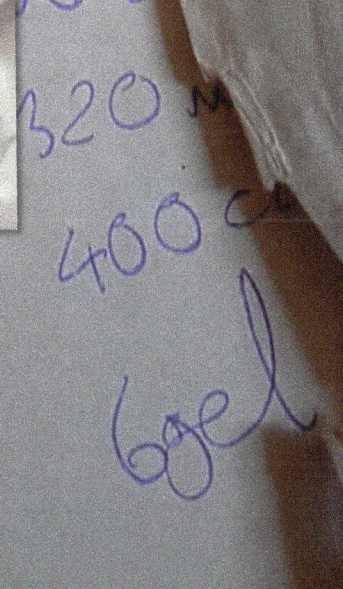

A relatively quick one to prepare, you first need to combine your sponge crumbs, golden syrup, sugar and melted dark chocolate to make a cookie dough. Next you need to add the scotch bonnet flavour. The amount you put in all depends on the particular chilli you have and amount of heat you can handle.

First, put the whole chilli into your smoothie blender with the olive oil and blend to a pulp. You may need to scrape the sides down a few times. Pass this through the finest sieve you have into a separate bowl. Take the chilli oil and add a couple of drops at a time to your cookie dough and knead well to full incorporate into the mix. Taste a tiny amount. Not enough heat? Add a couple more drops and repeat the process until you achieve the heat you want! As a ball park, about half the chilli oil should do, but this is personal preference. I'd say less is more here, as each cake will consist of a few bites. We're looking for an exciting bit of heat and scotch bonnet flavour without being overpowering.

Once you are happy with the flavour, weigh the dough and split it into 6 even portions. Shape each one by hand into the shape of a scotch bonnet chilli (best to have one in front of you for reference). I suggest using a fondant icing modelling tool to do the finer details. When you are happy, place them on a sheet of parchment and into the freezer for 2 hours.

An hour before you remove your cookie dough from the freezer, make your glaze. Soak your gelatine in cold water as usual. Heat the cream, milk and golden syrup in a small saucepan. When it's near the boil, add your squeezed out gelatine and chocolate and mix well. Take off the heat and add your olive oil. Transfer your glaze to a new bowl and, whisking constantly, add your food colouring a couple drops at a time. you are looking to match the colour of the scotch bonnet's flesh. Once achieved, cover your glaze in clingfilm and leave to cool, stirring every 10 minutes. when it reaches 31 degrees c it is perfect to use. This should take about an hour. Any hotter and it won't glaze, any colder and it will be globby. If it cools too much don't panic, simply heat in the microwave in 5 second bursts until around 50 degrees c, pass through a sieve and cool again. It should only take half the time to cool down compared to other recipes in this book as you are only making half as much.

When your cookie dough chillies are nice and firm, remove from the freezer and stick a cocktail stick in the stalk end of each one. Transfer your glaze to a narrow cup or glass and, one by one, dip your 'chillies' in the glaze, moving round to fully coat. Remove from the glaze and hold for around 15 seconds for the excess glaze to drain off, then stick the free end of the cocktail stick into the skin of the potato. Glaze all of your chillies, stick in your potato and transfer to the fridge.

In 30 minutes the glaze should have set and the dough should have softened. Remove each chilli from it's stick and insert a mint stalk into the hole that's left.

NOTE:

Always be careful when using chillies as you don't want to get any of the oil in your eyes! I suggest using disposable gloves as a precaution.

EGG CUSTARD PASTA WITH CHOCOLATE TRUFFLE

SERVES 6   This recipe will take you about 5 hours to complete.

INGREDIENTS

for the pasta:
- 6 egg yolks
- 3 whole eggs
- 90g double cream
- 60g sugar
- 9g vanilla essence (to taste)

for the truffle:
- 150g dark chocolate pellets
- 75g double cream
- 40g desiccated coconut
- cocoa powder, for dusting

for the foam:
- 200g fizzy orange soda
- 50g granulated sugar
- 1 sheet of gelatine

to garnish:
- 50g white chocolate chips (refrigerated)
- 24 small mint leaves

ADDITIONAL EQUIPMENT...

- small sauce pan
- hand whisk
- mixing bowl
- fine metal sieve
- dry pastry brush
- stick blender
- smoothie blender
- measuring jug
- 10" x 8" baking tray
- baking parchment
- sharp knife

First let's make the coconut truffle. Warm the cream in a small saucepan until bubbles just start forming round the edge. As soon as this happens pour into a mixing bowl that has the dark chocolate in and whisk until the chocolate is fully melted. Stir in the desiccated coconut and put in the fridge for 40 minutes to firm up slightly.

Once slightly firmed it's time to mould your truffles. You are looking to create a couple of odd shaped balls the same size and shape as truffles, the subterranean mushroom highly prized the world over. Once you are happy with the shape, leave in the fridge for a couple of hours. Better still, these can be made in advance and left overnight.

While the truffles are firming up you can make the orange foam. First soak the gelatine by submerging it in cold water. Take your orange soda and sugar and slowly heat it in a saucepan until the sugar is dissolved and it starts to boil. Immediately take it off the heat and whisk in the drained, squeezed out gelatine. Leave to cool for half an hour then refrigerate until needed.

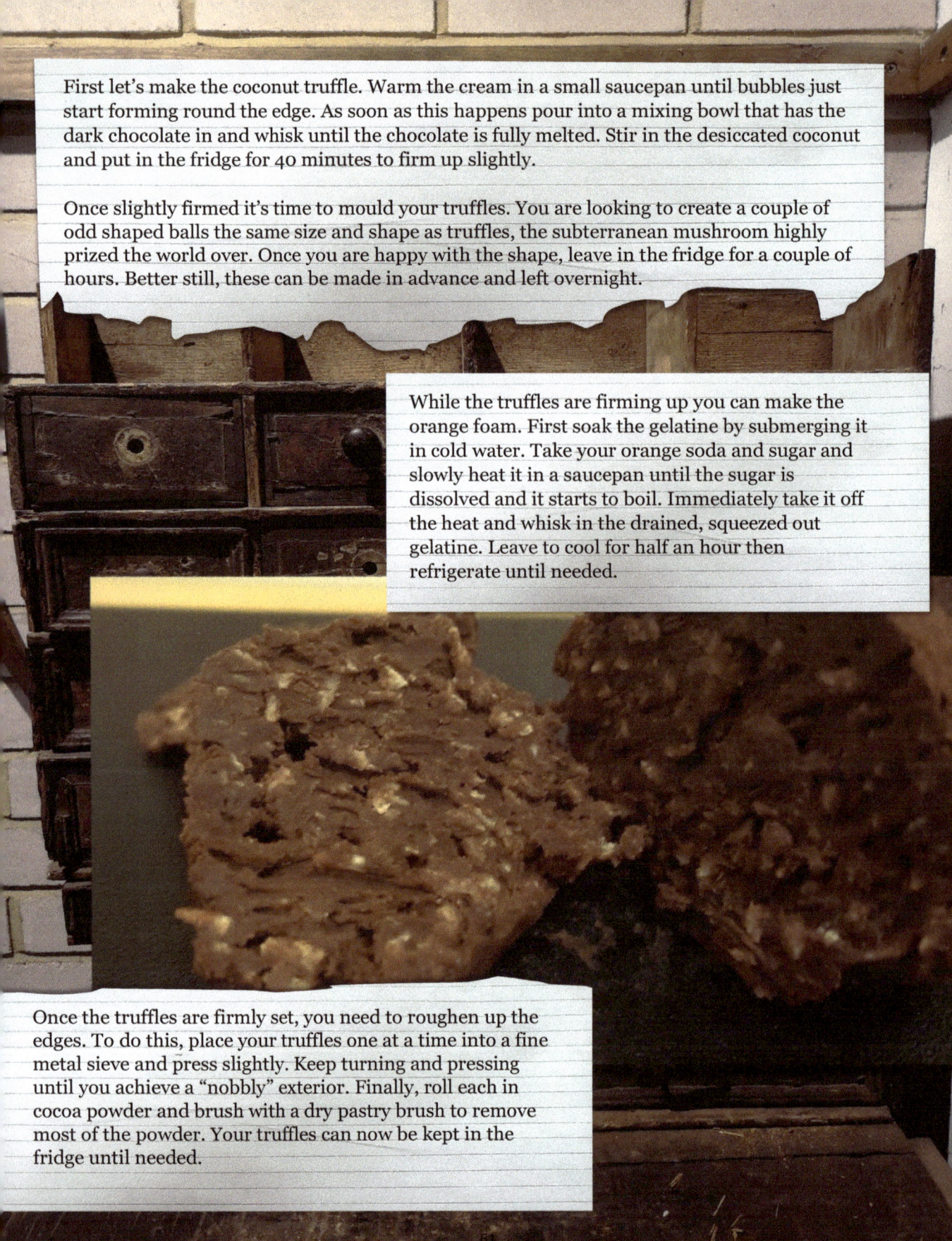

Once the truffles are firmly set, you need to roughen up the edges. To do this, place your truffles one at a time into a fine metal sieve and press slightly. Keep turning and pressing until you achieve a "nobbly" exterior. Finally, roll each in cocoa powder and brush with a dry pastry brush to remove most of the powder. Your truffles can now be kept in the fridge until needed.

The pasta is a little time consuming, but definitely worth it. Put all your ingredients into a smoothie blender and blend for one minute on high. Pour the mixture into a jug and leave for around 10 minutes. You are looking for the foam to settle on top, which then needs to be carefully skimmed off with a spoon and discarded. Removing the foam means that your "pasta" will not fluff up, but have a light consistency.

Take a 10" by 8" baking tray that is perfectly flat (to ensure an even thickness of pasta) and spread a small amount of oil around it with either a brush or some paper towel. Cut out a piece of baking parchment to fit the bottom of your tray and go up the sides just a little bit and press it onto your tray. Put this in a 170 degree C oven with no fan for 10 minutes to heat up.

When the tray is heated up, remove from the oven and, working quickly, pour 1/3 of your egg mix into the tray (weigh your mix after the skimming stage, then divide by 3) and swirl around with a circular motion to coat the bottom completely. Return to the oven for 4 minutes. After 4 minutes check your "pasta". If should be set and on its way to being dry but with hardly any brown colouration. If needed, leave in for a bit longer but check every minute without fail. When you are happy with the cooking, remove the parchment carefully from the tray and put straight into the fridge to chill. Repeat this process two more times from the start to cook the rest of your pasta then leave in the fridge for half an hour to cool down.

Before you are ready to plate, the final stage is your garnishes. Pick some small mint leaves out, 4 or 5 per portion should suffice. Put your refrigerated white chocolate chips into your smoothie blender and blitz for 10-15 seconds. You are looking to break the chocolate down so it resembles fine grated parmesan cheese, to a powder.

TO SERVE...

Take your egg custard pasta sheets out the fridge and, using a sharp knife, cut width ways into 5mm strips to resemble tagliatelle. Each sheet should give enough for 2 portions. Take a portion and swirl in the centre of a pasta bowl. Blitz your orange soda with a stick blender for 40 seconds. It should give off some foam. Spoon this off and pour onto your "pasta", a few spoonfuls for each dish. You will need to keep blending between each dish to generate more foam.

Next take your chocolate coconut truffle and slice into thin slices with the sharpest knife you own. It is best to do this straight from the fridge as it will give a cleaner cut. Place 3 or 4 truffle slices on top of each serving of pasta. A light dusting of white chocolate powder and a few mint leaves and you're ready to serve.

BEANS ON TOAST/ EGG ON TOAST

THE GRILLED LEMON SPONGE

MAKES 6 SLICES

INGREDIENTS

150g self raising flour
150g granulated sugar
150g melted butter
3 large eggs
zest of one lemon
juice of half a lemon
olive oil for brushing and grilling

ADDITIONAL EQUIPMENT...

8" by 4" loaf tin
baking parchment
pastry brush
electric or hand whisk
zester or fine grater
frying pan or griddle
mixing bowl

Preheat your oven to 165 degrees C. Whisk together all the ingredients apart from half the lemon juice until a nice, smooth batter is achieved.

Pour this batter into a parchment lined loaf tin measuring 8inches long by 4 inches across. Bake for 30 minutes. Insert a skewer into the centre of the cake and pull out. If there is no batter on the skewer the cake is cooked through. If some remains, bake for a bit longer.

As soon as you remove the cake from the oven, pour over the remaining lemon juice. Leave to cool for 2 hours.

Once cool slice slightly diagonally into 6 chunky slices.

One by one, brush each slice with olive oil and place on a hot frying pan or griddle, 6 seconds on each side. Not only does this give a more convincing "toast" appearance, it tastes amazing!

BEANS ON TOAST CAKE

MAKES 6 If your sponge is cooked, this will only take around 20 minutes.

INGREDIENTS

6 slices of grilled lemon sponge
125g ground almonds
125g icing sugar
1 egg white
juice from one orange
300g golden syrup
30g double cream
orange food colouring gel

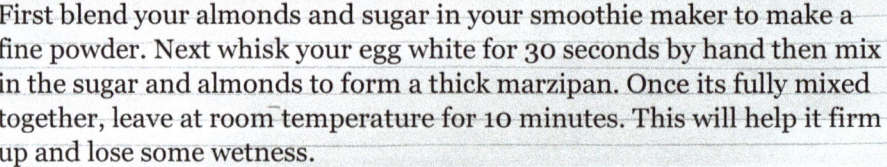

First blend your almonds and sugar in your smoothie maker to make a fine powder. Next whisk your egg white for 30 seconds by hand then mix in the sugar and almonds to form a thick marzipan. Once its fully mixed together, leave at room temperature for 10 minutes. This will help it firm up and lose some wetness.

Here comes the time consuming bit. Pick off small pieces of marzipan and roll into slightly flattened balls, exactly the shape and size of a baked bean. Continue until you have used all the marzipan (if you have too much you can always freeze for a later date).

Next mix your golden syrup and double cream with the juice from one orange until fully combined. Add the food colouring drop by drop until you have achieved the colour of baked bean sauce. Now add your marzipan "beans" to this liquid and stir gently. You are looking to coat the beans but retain their shape.

To serve, simply spoon the beans on top of your grilled sponge.

EGG ON TOAST CAKE

MAKES 6

This recipe will take around 10 minutes to prepare, providing you have your sponge made and grilled.

INGREDIENTS

6 slices of grilled lemon sponge

for the yolks:
 140g ripe mango flesh
 40g sugar

for the white:
 200g double cream
 90g icing sugar

This is possibly the easiest food illusion you can make. Take your mango flesh and blitz in a food processor with the sugar until completely smooth. Pour into a plastic squeezy bottle and chill until needed.

To make the 'egg white', whip the double cream with the icing sugar until it starts to thicken. You want to proceed slowly from here, as it can easily over whip. You want a consistency that will hold its shape, but still have a creaminess to it.

TO ASSEMBLE:

Take a slice of cake. Spoon and spread some of the cream onto it, the thickness and shape of a fried egg. Top with a squirt of the mango puree, in the shape of an egg yolk.

INGREDIENTS

for the yolk:

240g ripe mango flesh (after peeling and coring)
45g granulated sugar

for the pannacotta:

115g coconut milk
165g double cream
1/2 tsp vanilla extract
50g granulated sugar
1 and a half sheets of gelatine (6g)

for the "meat":

300g sponge cake crumbs
150g golden syrup
1 tsp ginger powder

for the crumb coating:

120g cornflakes
100g sugar syrup (page 31)

for the "black pudding":

45g white chocolate chips
150g sponge cake crumbs
75g dark chocolate melted
50g golden syrup

for the apple cream:

200g apple (after peeling and coring)
30g granulated sugar
10g double cream

ADDITIONAL EQUIPMENT...

1.5 inch half sphere silicone mould sheet (with at least 12 half spheres in it)
2 inch half sphere silicone mould sheet (with at least 12 half spheres in it)
sieve
smoothie maker
small saucepan
hand whisk
clingfilm
mixing bowl
3 inch diameter metal ring

DAY ONE

First you need to prepare the yolk and pannacotta, as these will need freezing overnight. Begin by chopping your mango flesh into small chunks. Put the mango, along with the sugar in your smoothie maker and blend for a good minute or so. You are looking for a smooth puree. Pass this through the finest sieve you own and into your 1.5 inch diameter half sphere moulds. You should get enough for 12 half spheres. Put the mould in the freezer for a good 3 hours.

Once the mango has frozen, you can make your pannacotta mix. Soak your gelatine in enough cold water to completely cover it and leave for 10 minutes. Meanwhile, combine the coconut milk, double cream, vanilla and sugar in a small saucepan and heat slowly, ensuring you stir it constantly. When you start to see bubbles around the edge add your drained and squeezed gelatine. Whisk the mix and strain through a fine sieve. Divide the mix between your 2 inch half sphere moulds, but make sure you don't fill completely; stop pouring around 3mm from the top.

Carefully unmould your mango half spheres and place one in each half sphere of pannacotta, as centrally as you can. Freeze overnight.

DAY TWO

This part will take you two hours to complete.

Time to prepare the "meat" for your scotch egg. Mix the sponge crumbs, golden syrup and ginger until fully incorporated to make cookie dough. Divide into six balls. Take one ball and flatten on a piece of clingfilm, to a thickness of around 2mm. Next you need to unmould two half spheres of frozen pannacotta and place together to make a full circle. Run your finger around the join a few times, just to create some stability then place this "egg" in the centre of the rolled out cookie dough. Bring the clingfilm up to wrap the dough around the pannacotta then remove the clingfilm. Working firmly but gently press the dough together, creating as perfect a sphere as you can. Repeat for the rest of and place in the freezer for 30 minutes to set.

Next, the crumb coating. I tested many different ingredients for this but the winner for texture, taste and visual appeal was the humble cornflake. Simply blitz them in your smoothie maker in 5 second bursts until they achieve the consistency of cooked bread crumbs. Take your scotch eggs out of the freezer and one by one, dip each into the sugar syrup, making sure it completely coats it. Remove from the syrup and allow any excess to drip off. Next roll each around in the cornflake crumbs to coat. Leave for 5 minutes then roll again in the crumbs to cover any parts you missed. When you have achieved an even coat, leave your "scotch eggs" out on the side for 1 hour to come up to temperature and allow the mango centre to turn to liquid.

While you are waiting, you can make the garnishes. For the black pudding, combine all the ingredients, ensuring the dark chocolate is melted but cool enough as to not melt the white chocolate chips. Divide the mix into 6 equal portions and push each one into a 3 inch diameter metal ring, to a thickness of about 1cm. Carefully remove the ring and repeat for the rest of the mixture. Place these in the fridge until needed.

For the apple cream, cut your apple into manageable chunks and place in a microwaveable container along with the sugar and cover. Microwave for 4 minutes on high. leave the apple to cool for about 15 minutes and then blitz in your smoothie maker (or food processor). Pass through a fine sieve and mix with the double cream until a smooth texture is achieved. Place somewhere cool until your pannacottas have come up to temperature.

TO PLATE...

Using a spoon, create 2 swooshes of apple cream on the plate. Place a piece of "black pudding" in the centre and finally, sit your pannacotta "scotch egg" on top.

STILTON CHEESECAKE

SERVES 2

You'll need about 3 hours and 15 minutes to make this dessert.

INGREDIENTS

for the cheesecake:

- 165g mascarpone
- 2 large egg
- 60g sugar
- ½ tsp vanilla
- 40g plain flour

for the mint syrup:

- 15 mint leaves
- 50g golden syrup
- 10g water
- blue food colouring (make sure it is bake proof)

for the shortbread:

- 65g cold butter
- 30g granulated sugar
- 90g plain flour

icing sugar for dusting

ADDITIONAL EQUIPMENT...

4" diameter by 2" high round cake tin (springform)
baking parchment
food processor
smoothie maker
squeezy bottle
a few sheets of kitchen roll
cocktail stick
piping bag
rolling pin
cookie tray
dry pastry brush

Start off by turning your oven on to 160 degrees C.

To make the cheesecake, whisk the cream cheese, egg, vanilla and sugar together until fully combined and smooth. Whisk the flour in until it is fully mixed in. Transfer this to a piping bag with a 1cm hole cut in the business end.

Line your small baking tin with baking parchment. Make sure you line both the bottom and the sides to avoid your cheesecake sticking.

Next you need to make your mint syrup. Put all the ingredients for it into your smoothie maker and blend until fully liquidised. Add food colouring until you take the green edge off and start to get a blue colour. Pass the syrup through a fine sieve into a squeezy bottle.

Take your lined cake tin and fill it 1 cm thick with cheesecake mix. Next you want to add dots of mint syrup randomly, yet not crowdedly. With your toothpick, pull through the mint syrup to create "veins" of colour. You don't need to go overboard at this stage. Repeat the process, 1 cm of cheesecake piped in, followed by the mint. when you near the top of the tin and only have 1 layers worth of cheesecake mix left to do, pipe it on as usual but don't add the mint syrup. Spread this layer smoothly with a palette knife then put into the centre of the oven for 30 minutes. It will puff up considerably in cooking. Remove from the oven and cool still in the tin for 30 minutes. Next, flip the tin over onto a piece of parchment and un clip, but leave the tin covering it and put in the fridge for 3 hours to firm up.

Whilst your cheesecake is cooking you can make your shortbread "crackers". Cube the butter and put into a food processor with the flour and sugar (this can be done in a bowl with and electric whisk if you don't have a food processor). Blitz until the mixture resembles breadcrumbs. Cut yourself two sheets of baking parchment at least 40cm by 40cm. Lay one of them on your work surface and empty your shortbread dough onto it. Press together with your hands to make a dough ball. Place the other sheet of parchment on top of this and press down with your hand to around an inch thick. Working up then across, roll the dough out to a thickness of around 3mm. Remove the top layer of parchment and cut the dough into seven squares each measuring 6 cm by 6 cm. Slide the parchment with the biscuits on onto a flat cookie tray and bake for 10 mins in the oven. Leave to cool on the tray.

Once your cheesecake has cooled, remove from the tin and dab with kitchen roll to remove any excess oil. Dust completely with icing sugar and brush off any excess. Serve on a board with the shortbread and a knife, cutting off wedges to top your shortbread as you would with stilton.

COFFEE AND WALNUT CAKE

MAKES 6

This will take two and a half hours to complete.

INGREDIENTS

for the sponge:

- 100g self raising flour
- 2 large eggs
- 100g butter, melted
- 1 shot of cold espresso
- 100g granulated sugar

for the coffee cream:

- 180g double cream
- 30g granulated sugar
- 1 shot of cold espresso

for the walnut filling:

- 60g walnuts, shelled
- 180g double cream
- 30g sugar

for the chocolate work:

- 360g good quality dark chocolate (55 percent cocoa content minimum)
- cocoa powder to dust

ADDITIONAL EQUIPMENT...

- 7 pieces of acetate measuring 9" by 2.75"
- six 2.25" diameter metal rings
- one 2" diameter metal ring
- 10" by 8" baking tin
- baking parchment
- piping bags
- fine metal sieve
- dry pastry brush
- electric whisk
- cookie tray
- blowtorch (optional)

TO MAKE THE COMPONENTS:

Preheat your fan oven to 170 degrees C. Start off by making the sponge, as this will need to cool down. Combine all the ingredients for the sponge and whisk to a smooth batter. Spread the mixture into a parchment lined baking tin, ensuring it's as level as possible. Bake for 10 minutes, or until a sharp knife inserted into the centre comes out clean. Remove from the oven and leave to cool completely in the tin (this should take around 1 hour).

Next for the coffee cream. Slowly whip the double cream with the sugar in a bowl until it starts to thicken. When it is thick enough to stand up on its own add the cold espresso and whisk very slowly until just combined. Transfer to a piping bag and refrigerate.

To make the walnut filling put the walnuts and sugar in your food processor and pulse a few times until the walnuts are broken to the size of rice grains. Whip the double cream in a separate bowl until thick and then fold in the walnuts and sugar. Transfer this to a piping bag and chill in the fridge.

When your sponge has completely chilled, remove from the tin, but keep the parchment underneath. Put another piece of parchment on top and press the flat side of the tin on top, to an even thickness (around 8mm). You can be quite firm, as the cake will spring back somewhat. Using the 2" pastry ring, cut 12 identical circles of sponge. The leftover sponge can be dried out and saved to make cookie dough for another recipe.

THE CHOCOLATE WORK:

Take six of your acetate sheets and lay them out on a clean surface. Temper your dark chocolate (page 24). Spread it over your acetate smoothly so you achieve a fairly thick, even coating. One by one, carefully roll the acetate strips so that they just fit inside a 2.25" metal ring. There will be overlap which will help to form a tight seal on the chocolate. If any chocolate shifts as you are putting the acetate in the ring, reapply with a thin knife or spatula. Once you have done all 6, place all of them standing up on a sheet of parchment which is on a cookie tray. Drop a small amount of chocolate into the bottom of each cylinder and tilt the tray to coat, creating a bottom to the cups. Put the tray into the fridge to set.

Put the leftover chocolate into a piping bag and cut a 3mm hole in the end. On your final piece of acetate pipe 6 "C" shapes roughly 2" tall and about 1cm thick. Try and make the bend as smooth as possible. Don't worry about making the ends neat, these can be trimmed. Place to set in the fridge once you are happy with the shape.

After around 30 minutes take the chocolate cylinders out of the fridge. Push the rings down firmly to break off any excess chocolate surrounding the bottom.

TO ASSEMBLE:

Take one of the chocolate cylinders still in its acetate and metal ring. Put a circle of the coffee sponge in the bottom. Next, pipe a layer of walnut mix 1cm thick, followed by 1 cm of coffee cream. Repeat with the sponge, making sure you gently push it down, then the walnut cream, followed finally by the coffee cream. Smooth the coffee cream till even. There should be a couple of mm left from the top. Repeat for the other five cups, returning each to the fridge as you go. Leave to chill in the fridge for 15 minutes.

Now to remove the acetate. Carefully slide the ring off, then slowly peel off the acetate. Turn a clean metal baking tin upside down and heat with your blowtorch for 30 seconds (this can be done in the oven if you don't have a blowtorch). Make sure you work on a non-flammable surface, on top of a turned off hob is ideal. Take a chocolate handle and press the ends onto the tin for a second or two until they melt to a uniform length. Stick this handle onto one side of each chocolate cup and hold in place to stick. Repeat for all your cakes then return to the fridge till serving, which should be as soon as possible.

To serve, dust with cocoa powder.

STICKS AND STONES

MAKES 6

This recipe will take around 3 and a half hours to prep, but you also need to allow an extra 15 minutes before serving to let the ganache and cookie stones soften up before serving.

INGREDIENTS

for the stones:

- 400g cake crumbs
- zest of 1 orange
- 75 g orange juice
- 75g golden syrup
- 200g white chocolate broken up into even pieces
- 20g oil
- black food colouring (you need the liquid for this recipe, not the gel)

for the ganache logs:

- 150g double cream
- 600g dark chocolate broken up
- cocoa powder, to dust

for the vanilla syrup:

- 120g sugar
- 120g water
- 3g vanilla extract

for the mint oil:

- good handful of mint leaves
- 30g olive oil

ADDITIONAL EQUIPMENT...

- baking parchment
- hand whisk
- at least 3 piping bags
- flat tray that will fit in your fridge
- dry pastry brush
- squeezy bottle (optional)
- smoothie maker
- cocktail sticks
- fine metal sieve

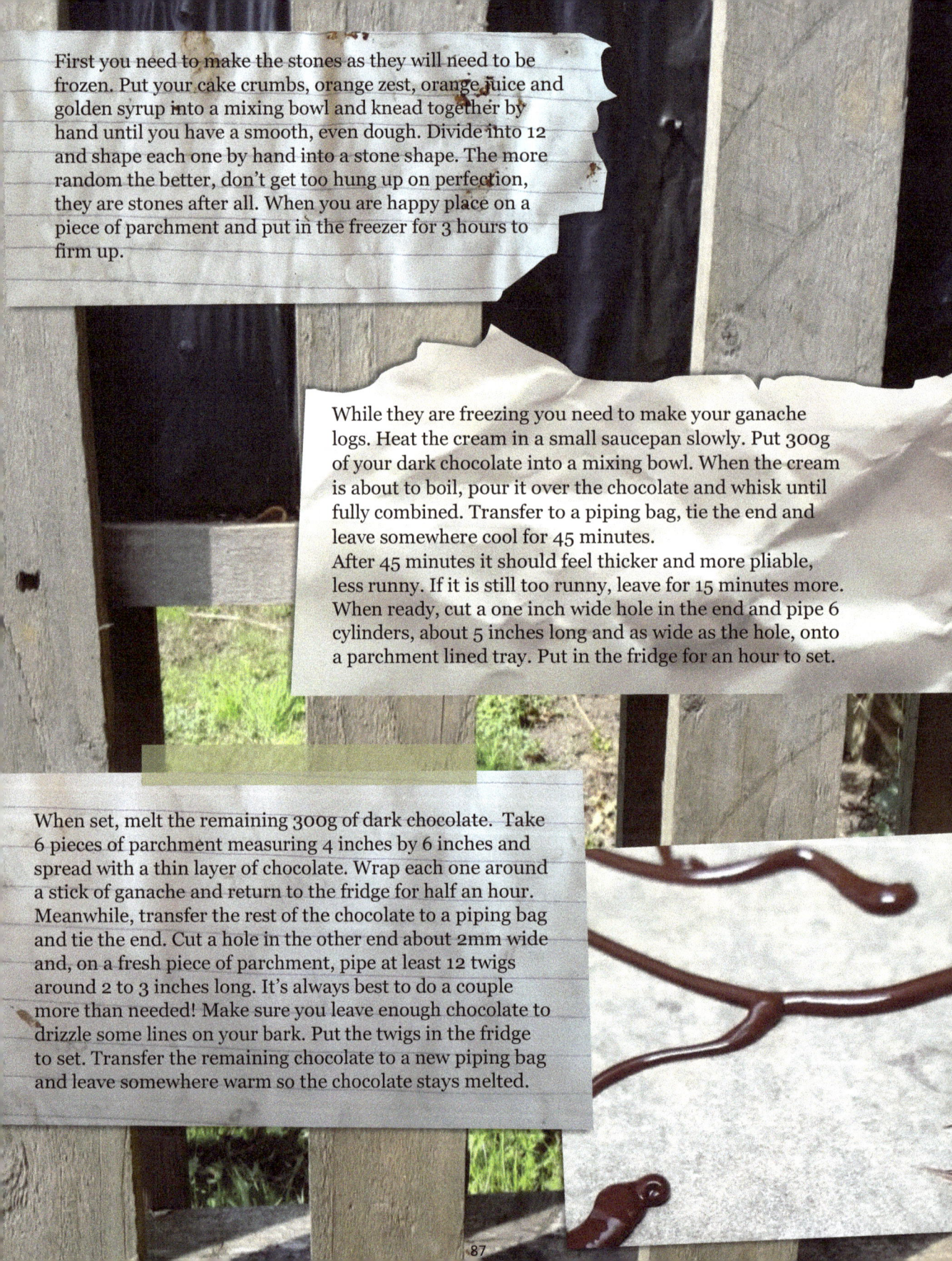

First you need to make the stones as they will need to be frozen. Put your cake crumbs, orange zest, orange juice and golden syrup into a mixing bowl and knead together by hand until you have a smooth, even dough. Divide into 12 and shape each one by hand into a stone shape. The more random the better, don't get too hung up on perfection, they are stones after all. When you are happy place on a piece of parchment and put in the freezer for 3 hours to firm up.

While they are freezing you need to make your ganache logs. Heat the cream in a small saucepan slowly. Put 300g of your dark chocolate into a mixing bowl. When the cream is about to boil, pour it over the chocolate and whisk until fully combined. Transfer to a piping bag, tie the end and leave somewhere cool for 45 minutes.
After 45 minutes it should feel thicker and more pliable, less runny. If it is still too runny, leave for 15 minutes more. When ready, cut a one inch wide hole in the end and pipe 6 cylinders, about 5 inches long and as wide as the hole, onto a parchment lined tray. Put in the fridge for an hour to set.

When set, melt the remaining 300g of dark chocolate. Take 6 pieces of parchment measuring 4 inches by 6 inches and spread with a thin layer of chocolate. Wrap each one around a stick of ganache and return to the fridge for half an hour. Meanwhile, transfer the rest of the chocolate to a piping bag and tie the end. Cut a hole in the other end about 2mm wide and, on a fresh piece of parchment, pipe at least 12 twigs around 2 to 3 inches long. It's always best to do a couple more than needed! Make sure you leave enough chocolate to drizzle some lines on your bark. Put the twigs in the fridge to set. Transfer the remaining chocolate to a new piping bag and leave somewhere warm so the chocolate stays melted.

After the logs have been setting for half an hour, remove from the fridge and make 2 small holes in each randomly with the end of a knife. This is where you will stick your twigs.
Cut a 1mm hole in the end of your piping bag and pipe a small amount of chocolate into each of the scalpel holes. Stick a twig in each, then drizzle a small amount of chocolate lengthways down each log for a bark effect. Once all are completed leave for 5 minutes then brush lightly with cocoa powder, being careful not to snap the twigs. Put your completed logs in the fridge until you are ready to serve.

The final thing to do while your stones freeze is to make the vanilla syrup. Simply put your water and sugar in a small saucepan and heat slowly until the sugar has dissolved. Take off the heat, stir in your vanilla and then leave to cool in a container or bowl for half an hour somewhere cool, then put in the fridge until needed.

The mint oil is even easier. Put your mint in your smoothie maker with the oil and blend for at 30 seconds. Strain through a fine sieve, ensuring no solids pass through. leave to one side until plate up.

Finally, your stones should be ready to finish (if it's been 3 hours since freezing).

Melt your white chocolate then whisk in the oil. Add the tiniest drop of black food colouring to give it a slight grey colour. Be very careful here as there's no way to undo too much colouring. Put this chocolate into a narrow mug or smoothie maker cup, as long as it is wide enough to allow you to dip your stones in. Prepare a large bowl or container of cold water alongside. Stick a cocktail stick into each stone.

Take your black food colouring and drip a couple of drops onto the top of your melted white chocolate. One by one, dip a "stone" into the white chocolate, pull out and wipe any excess on the bottom onto the rim of the cup. Slowly dip the stone into the cold water and hold, suspended for 15 seconds, then let drop to the bottom. After a few stones you may need to add a couple more drops of black colour to the chocolate as before. Remove all the stones from the water, pat dry with kitchen roll, and put in the fridge for 30 minutes to set.

TO ASSEMBLE:

You need to remove the ganache logs and cookie stones from the fridge 15 minutes before serving to allow them to soften a bit. First, spoon a couple of spoonful's of vanilla syrup into the bottom of a pasta bowl. Next position one of your logs in the middle of the bowl. Remove the cocktail sticks from your stones by carefully twisting and smooth over the hole with your finger, working quickly and briefly. Place two stones on the plate next to the log, then add a few dots of mint oil to the vanilla syrup, either with a squeezy bottle or spoon.

THE WASHING UP SPONGE

MAKES 8

You will need around 3 hours to complete this recipe.

INGREDIENTS

for the sponge:

- 200g self raising flour
- 4 medium eggs
- 200g olive oil
- 200g granulated sugar
- yellow gel food colouring

for the scourer top:

- zest of one lime
- 100g self raising flour
- 100g sugar
- 100g eggs
- 100g melted butter
- green gel food colouring

for the lemon foam:

- 100g sugar syrup
- 150g lemon juice
- 250g water
- 7g soya leitichin

for the baked apple coulis:

- 1 and a half granny smith apples
- 60g sugar
- 85g water
- 8g lemon juice
- green food colouring gel

ADDITIONAL EQUIPMENT...

- 8" by 10" baking tin
- stick blender
- baking parchment
- food processor
- stick blender
- fine sieve
- clean metal scourer
- Long shallow tupperware
- smoothie maker

First you need to make your sponge. Turn your oven to 170 degrees C. Put the eggs, sugar and flour into your food processor. Whizz on high speed for 2 minutes until you achieve a smooth, yet thick batter. You may need to scrape the sides of the bowl a couple of times. With the blade running, pour your olive oil through the feed hole into the mix. Then add the yellow food colouring a couple drops at a time until you achieve the same colour as a washing up sponge. Ensure the colour is fully mixed in then transfer the batter to your parchment lined baking tin and bake for 22 minutes, until a skewer comes out clean when stabbed into the centre of your cake. Remove the cake from the oven and place a sheet of parchment on top. Place a flat tray on top of this and flip the whole thing over. Leave to sit for 15 minutes, this will flatten the top of the sponge. Remove the original tin and leave to cool completely, for around 2 hours.

While your sponge is cooling you can make the rest of the components. To make the scourer top, put the lime zest, flour, sugar, eggs and butter into your food processor and blitz until completely liquidised. With the blade still running, add the green food colouring drop by drop until you achieve a deep green colour. Spread this mixture thinly into your parchment lined baking tin and bake for 4-5 minutes, it won't take long. Remove from the oven and allow to cool alongside your yellow sponge.

Next, the garnishes. To make the lemon foam put the sugar syrup, water, lemon juice and soya lecithin into a deep bowl. Blitz with your stick blender for around 2 minutes until the soya lecithin is completely dissolved. Transfer to a long, flattish tupperware, cover with clingfilm and put in the fridge. It needs to be as cold as possible to make a foam.

What is soya lecithin?

Soya lecithin is an emulsifier that gives stability to sauces, breads and other recipes. It is great for giving stability for when you want to make a foam, meaning your foam will hold for a good few minutes. It can be purchased from specialist ingredient shops, as well as on Amazon.

The last thing to make is your baked apple coulis 'washing up liquid'. Turn your oven up to 190 degrees c. Bake the half apple as it is for 30 minutes. Remove from the oven and leave to cool for half an hour. When it has cooled a bit, blend in your smoothie maker with 60g of the sugar and 60g water. Blend to a smooth puree and pass through a fine sieve.

Clean out your smoothie maker then put in the other apple that has been chopped up, 25g water and 8g lemon juice. Blend for around a minute and pass through your fine sieve into the baked apple puree. Whisk to fully mix then refrigerate until needed.

TO ASSEMBLE THE SPONGE:

Take your cooled lime sponge and break up into pieces. Put into your food processor and blitz until completely crumbed. Leave to one side.

Slightly trim your yellow olive oil sponge on all four sides and the top so you have a neat rectangle with a flat top. Divide it into 8 equal rectangles by cutting once lengthways and 3 times width ways. Top each with a layer of green crumb, about 3mm thick, and compress firmly to make dense. Trim the edges to make neat and roughen up the top a bit with your clean metal scourer.

TO PLATE:

Place one of your sponges on a plate, green side up, ensuring the green crumb stays in place. Add a spoonful of your baked apple coulis onto the top of your sponge, allowing it to carefully run down one side (a squeezy bottle is ideal for this). Finally, take your lemon foam out of the fridge. Fold back the clingfilm, place your stick blender into the mix and wrap the clingfilm back over so there are no gaps. Blend the mix, keeping the blades just under the surface of the liquid. Within a minute you will see bubbles forming. Keep blending until you have enough bubbles. You may need to blend again between each plating. Spoon a couple of spoonful's onto one edge of your sponge and serve immediately.

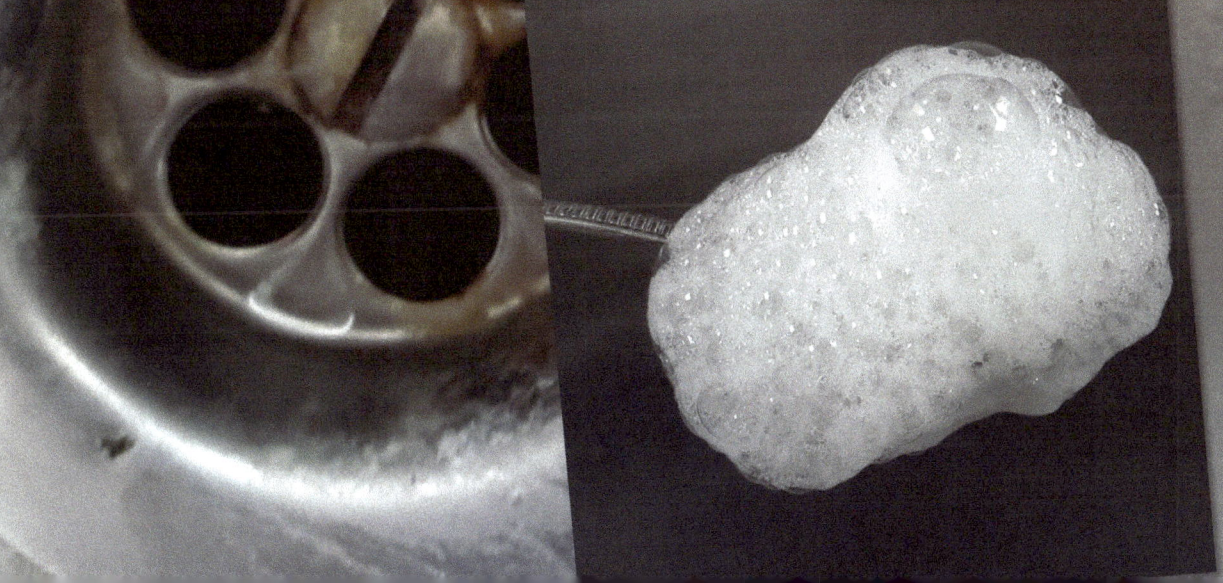

450g butter
100g white sugar
170g brown sugar
1 tsp salt

PIZZA CAKE

MAKES A 10" DIAMETER CAKE

This is a relatively straight forward recipe and should take around one hour and 45 minutes to complete.

for the base:
150g self raising flour
150g granulated sugar
150g butter
3 medium eggs
1 teaspoon vanilla extract

for the sauce:
120g strawberry jam

for the "cheese":
150g refrigerated white chocolate chips

for the "pepperoni":
20g strawberry jam
red food colouring gel
45g ground almonds
15g granulated sugar
25g icing sugar

ADDITIONAL EQUIPMENT...

big oven tray that fits in your freezer
10" springform cake tin
8" springform cake tin base
electric whisk
cling film
baking parchment
blowtorch

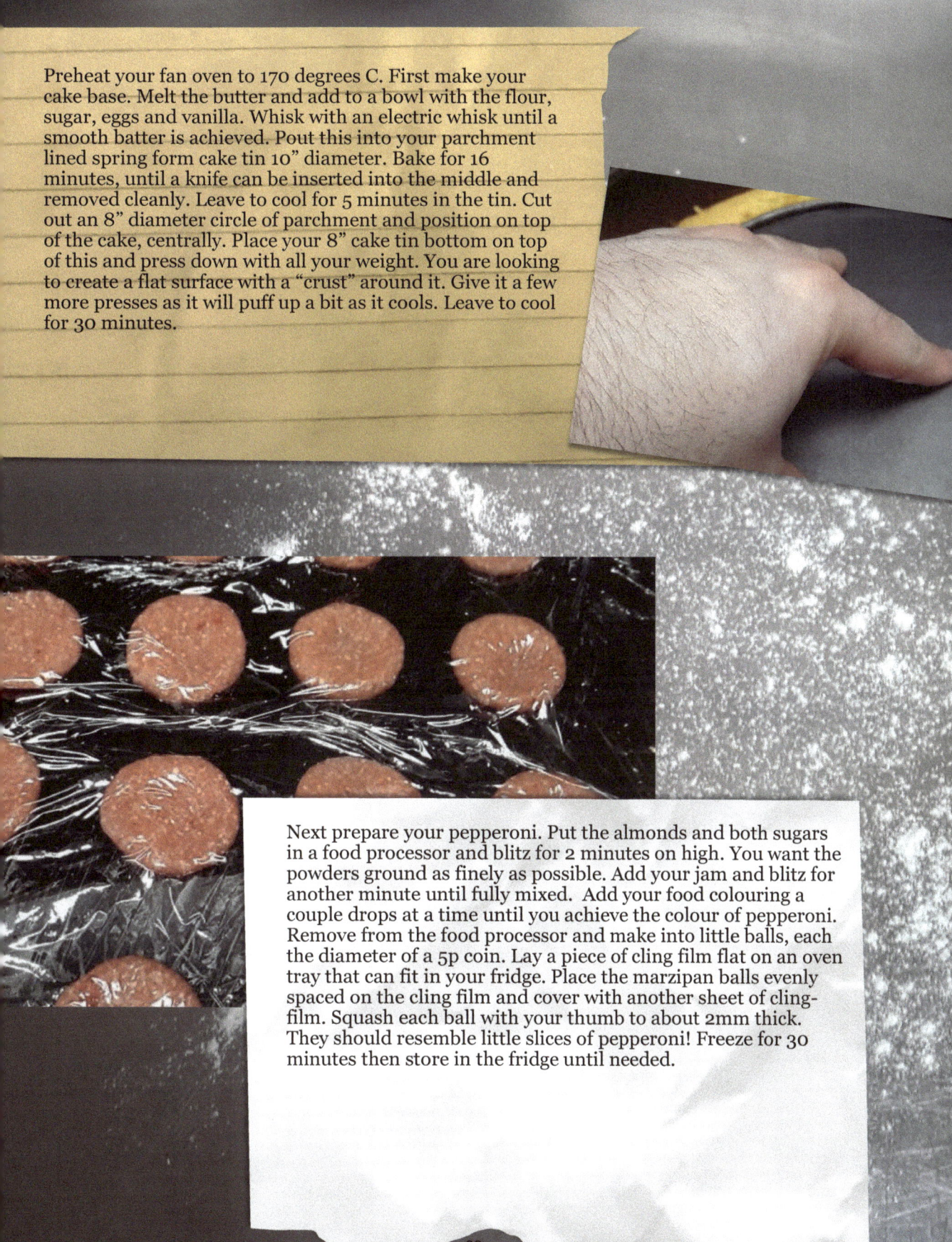

Preheat your fan oven to 170 degrees C. First make your cake base. Melt the butter and add to a bowl with the flour, sugar, eggs and vanilla. Whisk with an electric whisk until a smooth batter is achieved. Pout this into your parchment lined spring form cake tin 10" diameter. Bake for 16 minutes, until a knife can be inserted into the middle and removed cleanly. Leave to cool for 5 minutes in the tin. Cut out an 8" diameter circle of parchment and position on top of the cake, centrally. Place your 8" cake tin bottom on top of this and press down with all your weight. You are looking to create a flat surface with a "crust" around it. Give it a few more presses as it will puff up a bit as it cools. Leave to cool for 30 minutes.

Next prepare your pepperoni. Put the almonds and both sugars in a food processor and blitz for 2 minutes on high. You want the powders ground as finely as possible. Add your jam and blitz for another minute until fully mixed. Add your food colouring a couple drops at a time until you achieve the colour of pepperoni. Remove from the food processor and make into little balls, each the diameter of a 5p coin. Lay a piece of cling film flat on an oven tray that can fit in your fridge. Place the marzipan balls evenly spaced on the cling film and cover with another sheet of clingfilm. Squash each ball with your thumb to about 2mm thick. They should resemble little slices of pepperoni! Freeze for 30 minutes then store in the fridge until needed.

Next take your white chocolate and pulse in your smoothie blender until crumbled up, the finer the better. This must be done from fridge cold or you will just get a sludgy mess. Chocolate chips work best for this as they are small enough to blend quickly.

Finally, take your jam and whisk in a bowl until it becomes runny, half a minute with an electric whisk should do it.

TO ASSEMBLE:

Spread the jam on your cake base, but make sure you don't get any on the crust. Next evenly sprinkle the white chocolate on top of the jam. Be generous as it will shrink as it heats. Place your cake back into the oven for 5 minutes to melt the chocolate and heat through.

Remove your cake from the oven and fire up your cook's blowtorch. torch the chocolate gently, being careful not to burn any. This should give you a nice caramelised taste and authentic pizza look.

Place your "pepperoni" on top as you would a pizza, remove from the tin and serve while still warm.

THE CHOCOLATE BROWNIE TREE

MAKES 8

This recipe will take you roughly 5 hours from start to serving.

INGREDIENTS

for the brownie:
5 medium eggs
410g granulated sugar
130g plain flour
60g cocoa powder
250g butter
250g dark chocolate, broken into small pieces

for the maple filling:
240g maple syrup

for the ganache:
160g white chocolate chips or broken up pieces
60g double cream

for the chocolate work:
350g dark chocolate

to garnish:
25g lemon balm leaves (left out over night to dry out)
50g granulated sugar
cocoa powder to dust

ADDITIONAL EQUIPMENT...

at least 3 piping bags
10" by 8" oven tray
hand whisk
baking parchment
fine sieve
scalpel
spatula
dry pastry brush
smoothie blender

This recipe needs to be started at least 5 hours before serving. First, to make the brownie. Turn your fan oven to 170 degrees C. Melt the butter on a low heat in a small saucepan. Once it is all melted add your broken up dark chocolate and whisk by hand until fully combined. Set this aside.

In a mixing bowl whisk the eggs and sugar together until creamy and pale, about a minute by hand should suffice. Sieve in your flour and cocoa powder and give it a whisk. Finally add your butter and chocolate mix and whisk the whole thing together until smooth. Transfer the mix to your 10" x 8" baking tray lined with parchment and bake for 22 minutes. The brownie will still be a bit gooey in the middle but to test if it is done, give the tray a shake. If there is no wobble it is cooked. If you get a slight wobble, leave for 5 minutes more. Once your brownie is cooked remove from the oven and leave somewhere cool for around 2 hours.

Once your brownie is cool, trim about 1 cm off each edge (this can be kept for soil for another recipe! Cut the brownie slab down the middle lengthways and three times horizontally into 8 equal rectangles. This is where it gets messy...Take a piece of brownie and knead with your hand. You want to make it into a smooth doughy mess so get stuck in and mould it thoroughly. Once happy with the texture shape it into a sausage shape 1.5" in diameter. Take your scalpel and push the handle end into one end of the brownie "sausage", but don't push all the way through. Leave a couple of centimetres. You want to wiggle it in small circular motions to open the hole up slightly, but be careful to not breach the outside. Repeat for the rest of the brownie pieces and place in the freezer on a parchment lined tray for around half an hour.

While they are firming up, make your ganache. Heat the cream in a small saucepan until nearly boiling and add the white chocolate, whisking until fully melted. Take this of the heat and leave to cool, for 15 minutes, stirring every 5 minutes.

Next, cut out 16 pieces of baking parchment to wrap around each brownie "log". The best way to do this is wrap your parchment around one of the logs and cut, leaving 1 cm longer for breathing room. Cut again so it is the length of the brownie plus 1 cm. Use this as a template to cut 15 more parchment pieces. Put 8 of these to one side. Take the remaining parchment and spread each one with your ganache, to the thickness of around 1mm. One by one, wrap your brownies up so they are coated in ganache and leave the parchment on. Place in the freezer for 20 minutes to set.

Now you can melt the chocolate for the coating, either in a bain marie or in the microwave. You don't need to worry too much about tempering for this recipe. Take your 8 reserved parchment rectangles and screw up in your hands, then flatten out again.

Spread each one with some melted chocolate using your spatula. Working quickly but carefully, remove the parchment from your ganache coated logs and re wrap each one in the chocolate parchment, ensuring complete coverage. Lay these carefully in the fridge for 20 minutes to set.

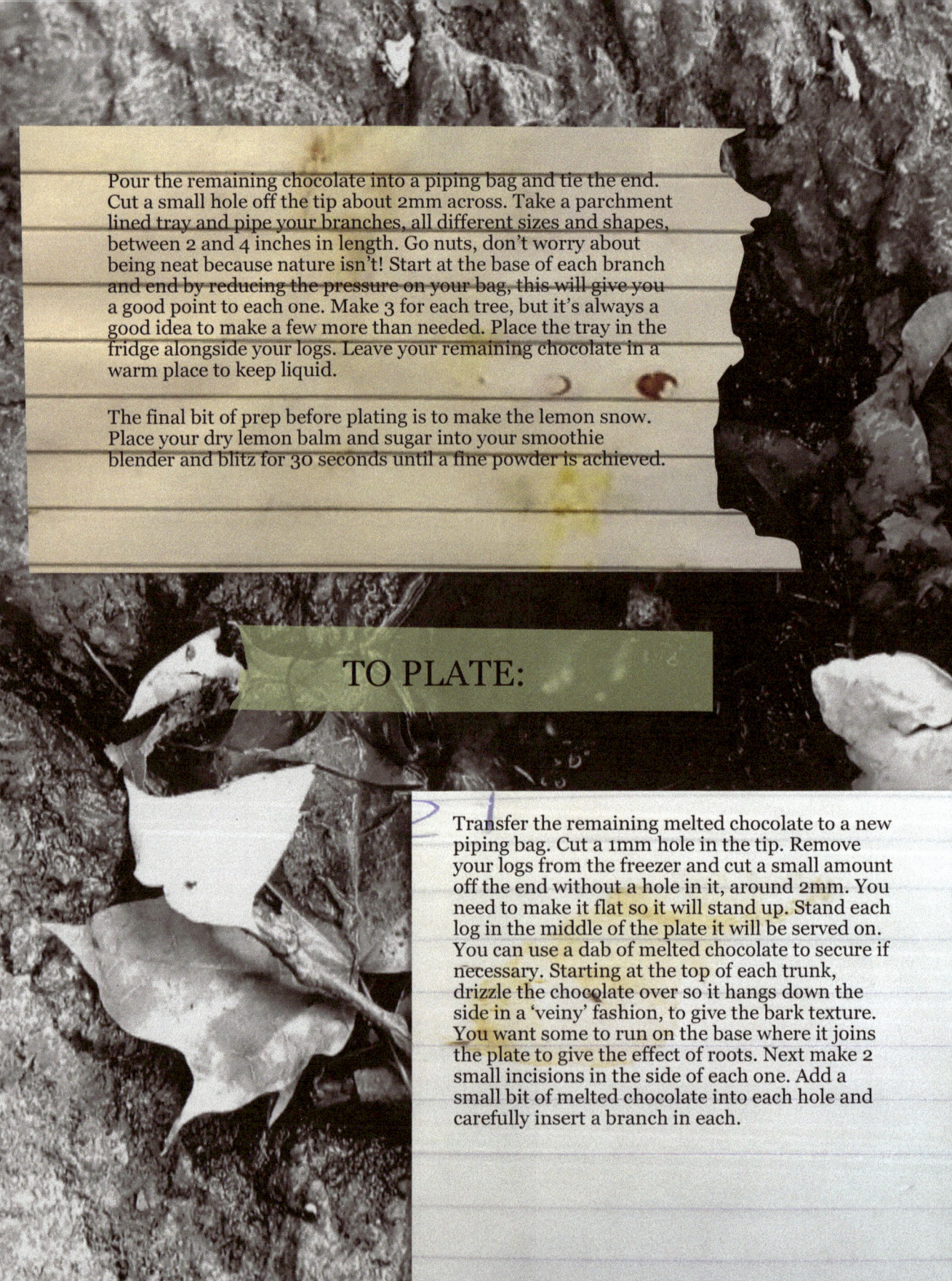

Pour the remaining chocolate into a piping bag and tie the end. Cut a small hole off the tip about 2mm across. Take a parchment lined tray and pipe your branches, all different sizes and shapes, between 2 and 4 inches in length. Go nuts, don't worry about being neat because nature isn't! Start at the base of each branch and end by reducing the pressure on your bag, this will give you a good point to each one. Make 3 for each tree, but it's always a good idea to make a few more than needed. Place the tray in the fridge alongside your logs. Leave your remaining chocolate in a warm place to keep liquid.

The final bit of prep before plating is to make the lemon snow. Place your dry lemon balm and sugar into your smoothie blender and blitz for 30 seconds until a fine powder is achieved.

TO PLATE:

Transfer the remaining melted chocolate to a new piping bag. Cut a 1mm hole in the tip. Remove your logs from the freezer and cut a small amount off the end without a hole in it, around 2mm. You need to make it flat so it will stand up. Stand each log in the middle of the plate it will be served on. You can use a dab of melted chocolate to secure if necessary. Starting at the top of each trunk, drizzle the chocolate over so it hangs down the side in a 'veiny' fashion, to give the bark texture. You want some to run on the base where it joins the plate to give the effect of roots. Next make 2 small incisions in the side of each one. Add a small bit of melted chocolate into each hole and carefully insert a branch in each.

Put the maple syrup in a piping bag and tie the end well. Cut a small hole in the business end and fill each tree up in the hole that was made at the start with your scalpel handle. Drizzle the top of each tree with the remaining chocolate and insert a third branch, making sure it comes out at an angle. Go back to the first tree (the chocolate should have started to set) and brush with the tiniest amount of cocoa powder, being careful not to dislodge the branches. Repeat for the rest of your trees.

The finishing touch before serving is to sieve over some of your lemon balm sugar, creating an eerie snowfall...

CHOCOLATE ORANGE YULE LOG

MAKES 4

This recipe will need to be started a day in advance as the flat mousse needs to be frozen overnight.

INGREDIENTS

for the flat mousse filling:
- 100g double cream
- 90g freshly squeezed orange juice
- 2 sheets of gelatine (8g)
- 50g dark chocolate, broken up into small pieces
- zest of 1 orange

for the sponge:
- 4 large eggs, separated
- 100g granulated sugar
- 20g cocoa powder

for the ganache:
- 40g double cream
- 80g dark chocolate

for the chocolate work:
- 200g dark chocolate
- cocoa to dust

the garnishes
for the moss:
- 15 large leaves of mint
- 15g vanilla sponge crumbs
- 25g granulated sugar
- green food colouring gel

ADDITIONAL EQUIPMENT...

- silicone spatula
- at least 3 disposable piping bags
- small oven tray (that can fit in your freezer)
- baking parchment
- 10" x 8" oven tray
- cling film
- smoothie blender
- dry pastry brush

DAY ONE

This recipe needs to be started a day in advance, as the centre needs to be frozen. To make the flat mousse, first soak your gelatine by covering it completely with cold water. Warm the orange juice and zest in a small saucepan. When bubbles start to appear at the edge, add your drained and squeezed gelatine and dark chocolate and whisk to combine. Take off the heat and leave to cool at room temperature for about an hour, stirring every 10 minutes or so. While you wait, whisk your double cream to stiff peaks in a separate bowl, being careful not to over whisk.

Once your chocolate orange mix has cooled enough, loosely fold it into the whipped cream, then lightly whisk the mix with a hand whisk to fully combine, but ensure the mixture maintains its whipped state. Transfer this flat mousse to a piping bag and cut a 2cm wide hole in the business end. As neatly as you can, pipe four straight cylinders 5 inches long and 2 cm thick onto a parchment lined tray. Place this tray in the freezer overnight to set.

DAY TWO

Heat your fan oven to 170 degrees c. To make the sponge, beat together your egg yolks, sugar and cocoa powder until smooth and glossy. In a clean bowl whisk your egg whites to stiff peaks. Continue whisking and add in your chocolate yolk mix. Whisk until fully combined but don't overdo it. Working quickly, pour this batter into your parchment lined baking tray, spreading evenly. Bake for 6 minutes until just cooked. Leave to cool for one hour.

While the sponge is cooling you can make your ganache. Heat the double cream in a small saucepan until just boiling then add your broken up dark chocolate, stirring constantly until completely melted. Leave this to one side to cool slightly for 30 minutes. Now to start assembling…

Start by cutting out 4 pieces of baking parchment, each measuring 6" by 5". Spread each one with an even layer of ganache. Cut your sponge into 4 rectangles, each measuring 4" by 5"and lay one on top of each rectangle of ganache. lay a frozen mousse cylinder on each rectangle lengthways and then bring the parchment around to create an even roll (almost like an artic roll). Wrap each in clingfilm to secure. Place your 4 packages in the freezer for 15 minutes to harden slightly.

Next melt your chocolate slowly in a bain marie. Once it has melted, pour into a piping bag and secure the end with a length of string (I use cling film made into a string). Cut a 2mm hole in the other end and pipe eight branch shapes onto a sheet of baking parchment. Each should measure between 2 to 4 inches. I always pipe more than I need as some come out better than others. Set these in the fridge to cool until needed.

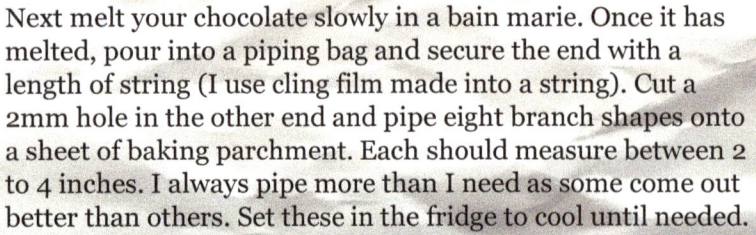

Next cut out four rectangles of baking parchment 6" by 5". Screw each one up in your hand then un-scrunch again. Pipe some chocolate onto each and spread in a thin layer. Working quickly, unwrap each of your frozen sponge rolls and place one onto each chocolate coated parchment sheet lengthways. Roll the baking parchment around each log, not worrying about neatness. Again, return these to the fridge for 15 minutes. Remember to leave your remaining chocolate somewhere warm to keep melted.

Remove your logs from the fridge and take off the baking parchment. Next you are looking to create texture and attach the twigs. Transfer your chocolate to a new piping bag and this time make a 1mm hole in the end. Working lengthways, drizzle the chocolate in a thin stream up and down each chocolate log to create a bark effect. Next make two small holes in your log at random places and pipe a small amount of chocolate in. stick a "twig" in each hole then again return to the fridge for another 15 minutes.

Nearly there! For the finishing touch you need to make some moss. Place the mint, crumbs and sugar in your smoothie blender and blitz. You may need to scrape the mixture down a few times. Add some green food colouring a couple drops at a time until you achieve a light moss colour. When happy, crumble the mixture a bit with your fingers to separate.

To finish your logs, brush each with cocoa powder, removing excess by smoothing with your finger. This will also give an interesting colour contrast on the surface. Add a small amount of "moss" to each log, leave out for a final 15 minutes to come up to temperature then serve.

THE CHOCOLATE THRONE

This recipe will take around four and a half hours to complete.

MAKES 4

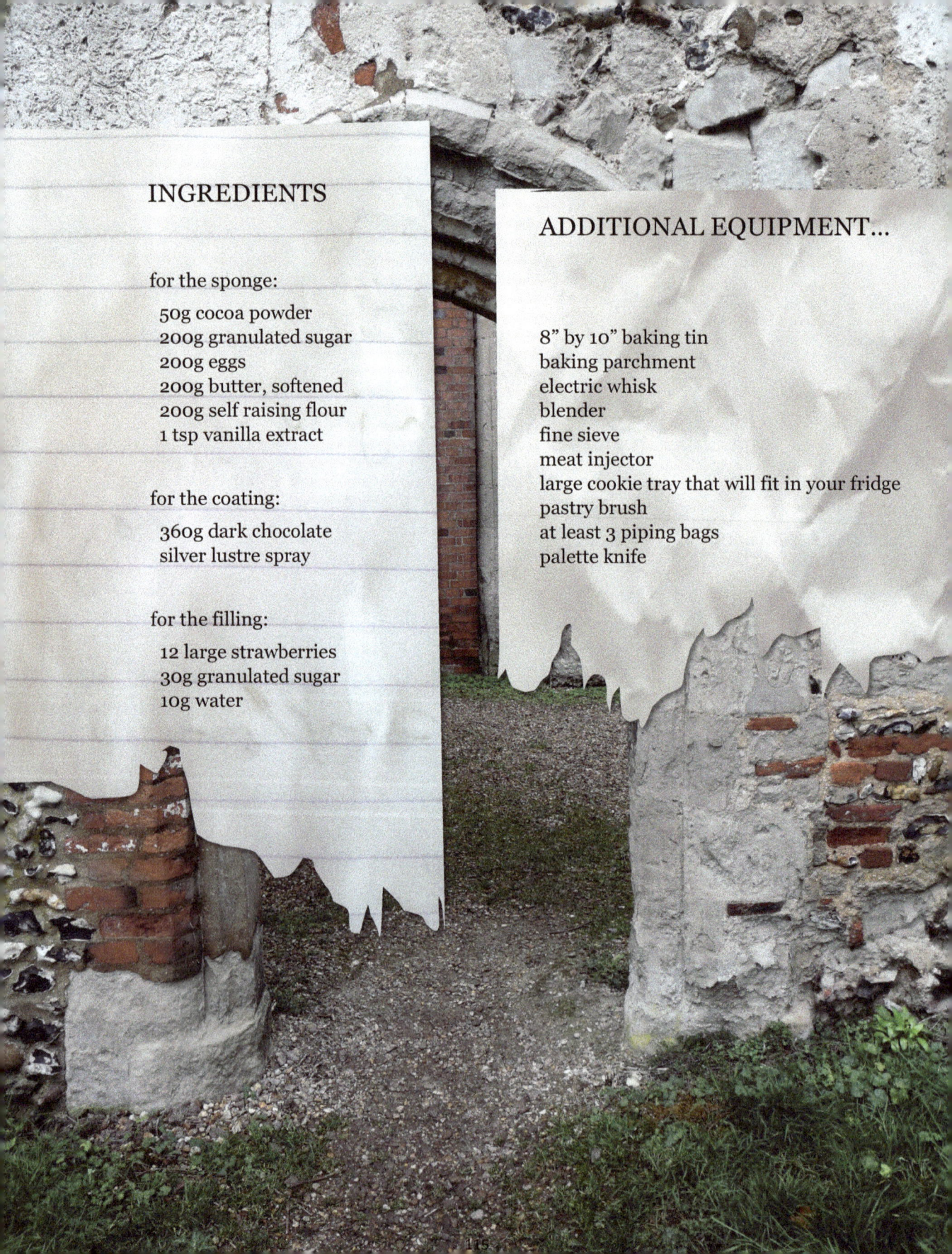

INGREDIENTS

for the sponge:

50g cocoa powder
200g granulated sugar
200g eggs
200g butter, softened
200g self raising flour
1 tsp vanilla extract

for the coating:

360g dark chocolate
silver lustre spray

for the filling:

12 large strawberries
30g granulated sugar
10g water

ADDITIONAL EQUIPMENT…

8" by 10" baking tin
baking parchment
electric whisk
blender
fine sieve
meat injector
large cookie tray that will fit in your fridge
pastry brush
at least 3 piping bags
palette knife

First start by making the cake. Heat your fan oven to 170 degrees C. Cream together the sugar and butter with an electric whisk for around 3 minutes until full combined and it starts to go fluffy. Add the vanilla. Next whisk the eggs in one by one, followed by the flour and cocoa powder. Keep whisking until you achieve a smooth chocolate cake batter. Pour the batter into your parchment lined baking tin and spread out evenly. Bake for around 24 minutes, ensuring a skewer inserted comes out clean. Once cooked, remove from the oven and run a butter knife between the cake and tin then flip onto a baking parchment lined chopping board. Remove the baking tin and place the tin on top of the cake, flat side down to flatten slightly. Leave to cool like this for 2 hours.

While the sponge is cooling, you can make your coulis. Put the strawberries, sugar and water into your blender and blitz on high until completely liquidised. Pass your coulis through a fine sieve and store in the fridge until needed.

TO CUT THE SPONGE...

First, cut the four sides off your sponge so it measures 8" by 6".

Next, cut the sponge into four oblongs each measuring 2" by 6".

Turn the four oblongs on their side and trim off the curved top edge so they each measure 1" thick.

Take one 2" by 6" oblong and cut in half so you have two pieces each measuring 2" by 3".

Take one of these rectangles and cut a smaller rectangle out the centre measuring 1.5" long by 0.75" across. Discard the cut-out part.

Take the other 2" by 3" piece of sponge and cut so you have two pieces, one piece 2" by 2" and the other 2" by 1".

Cut the 2" by 1" piece in half lengthways so you have two pieces measuring 2" by 1" by 0.5". Discard one of them.

Nearly there! Take the piece measuring 2" by 2" and cut in half like so.

The final stage is to cut each one of these pieces diagonally, through the top as shown, so the top face measures 0.5" by 2" and the bottom face measures 1" by 2". Discard the small cut-off.

Once you have all your pieces cut out, repeat for the remaining three oblongs of sponge so you have enough parts to make four thrones.

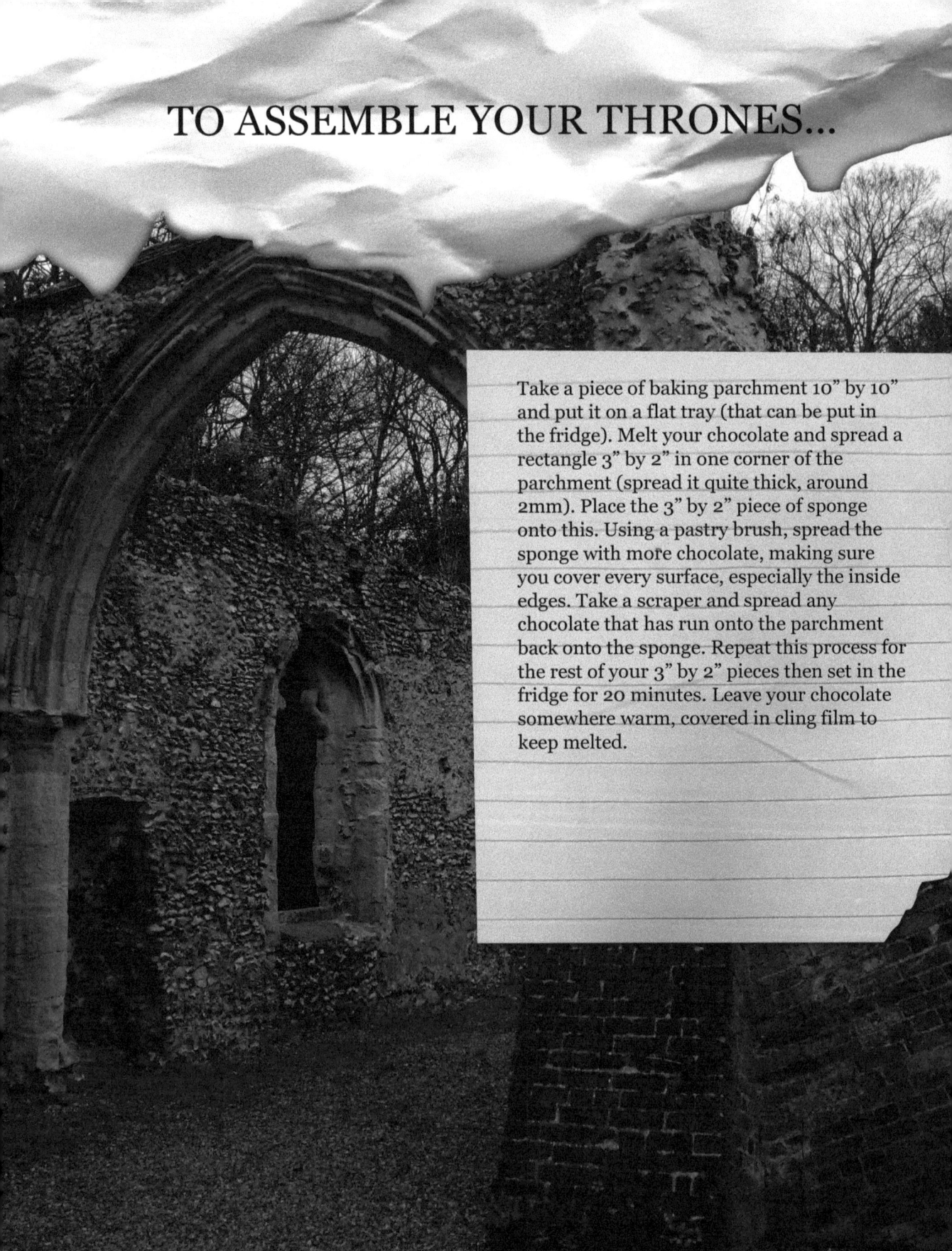

TO ASSEMBLE YOUR THRONES...

Take a piece of baking parchment 10" by 10" and put it on a flat tray (that can be put in the fridge). Melt your chocolate and spread a rectangle 3" by 2" in one corner of the parchment (spread it quite thick, around 2mm). Place the 3" by 2" piece of sponge onto this. Using a pastry brush, spread the sponge with more chocolate, making sure you cover every surface, especially the inside edges. Take a scraper and spread any chocolate that has run onto the parchment back onto the sponge. Repeat this process for the rest of your 3" by 2" pieces then set in the fridge for 20 minutes. Leave your chocolate somewhere warm, covered in cling film to keep melted.

Once the chocolate coating has set take a fresh piece of baking parchment the same size, 10" by 10". Again, spread a rectangle of chocolate 3" by 2" and place a chocolate coated piece of cake onto this, open side down this time. Scrape the chocolate back onto it as before, repeat for the other three pieces and return to the fridge. What you should have is chocolate coated sponges with a cavity in the middle.

Transfer the remaining chocolate to a piping bag and tie the end. On a final piece of baking parchment you need to pipe swords of chocolate. Cut a 2mm hole in the end of the piping bag and pipe quite thick, straight lines of chocolate measuring roughly 3" long. Pipe a smaller line ½" in length across each "blade" near one end (like a sword handle). You will need around 30 of these, but best to do a couple extra just in case. Set these in the fridge for around 20 minutes.

Using some of the remaining chocolate, attach the base and arms to the back as shown. Hold in place for a few seconds to set and repeat for the other three. Place in the fridge on baking parchment to set for 20 minutes to set.

Take a final piece of baking parchment and pipe a fan of straight lines of chocolate roughly 4 inches long as shown. Place your throne back side down onto the fan of chocolate.

Transfer your remaining chocolate to a new piping bag and cut a 1mm hole in the end. Drizzle chocolate up and down your thrones. Attach six swords to the back rest of each throne then drizzle more chocolate up and down each throne, covering the arms, back and side. Return to the fridge for a final time to set for 20 minutes before serving.

TO SERVE:

THE MEAT INJECTOR:

Meat injectors can be picked up relatively cheaply. While usually used for basting and tenderising meat, I've found it perfect for getting the strawberry coulis into the centre of the chocolate throne.

Fill your meat injector with strawberry coulis, ensuring the thickest syringe is attached (around 2mm thick). Stand each throne up and spray with your silver lustre to completely coat. One at a time, insert the needle of the meat injector into the top of each throne, ensuring it reaches into the inside cavity. Slowly inject about 15 ml into the centre of each one and serve straight away. Encourage the eater to bring their knife down straight through the centre, causing the throne to bleed its strawberry centre.

THE ASHTRAY PANNACOTTA

MAKES 6 This recipe should take you around 3 and a half hours, from start to finish.

INGREDIENTS

for the pannacotta:
 460g double cream
 80g caster sugar
 3 sheets of gelatine (12g)
 dash of vanilla essence

for the smoky lapsang gel:
 2 smoky lapsang teabags
 380g water
 60g caster sugar
 5g agar agar

for the meringue:
 2 egg whites
 50g icing sugar
 50g caster sugar
 good quality black food colouring gel

for the chocolate crumb:
 80g dark chocolate pellets, frozen
 4g silver lustre powder

for the cigarette butts:
 60g white chocolate
 30g icing sugar
 orange food colouring gel
 small bar of white chocolate, chilled

ADDITIONAL EQUIPMENT...

electric whisk
6 clean, brand new ashtrays 75mm across by 30mm tall
fine grater
squeezy bottle or piping bag
smoothie blender

FOR THE PANNACOTTA:

Start off by soaking your gelatine in enough cold water to cover it. Next, heat the cream, sugar and a dash of vanilla extract in a small saucepan until just boiling, whisking while you do so. Remove your gelatine and squeeze out all water, then whisk into your cream mixture until fully dissolved. Transfer your mix to a jug and pour into each of your ashtrays, about 15mm deep. Put in the fridge to set for around 3 hours.

FOR THE MERINGUE ASH:

While the pannacotta is setting you can make the meringue 'ash'. First heat your oven to 90 degrees C. In a clean bowl, whisk your egg whites to stiff peaks. Mix both your sugars together in a separate bowl. While still whisking your egg whites at high speed add a tablespoon of sugar at a time until the meringue is thick and glossy and you've used all the sugar. Finally whisk in some black food colouring gel a drop at a time until you get a dark grey colour. It's important to use a good quality gel as you need the meringue to stay thick and glossy. Spread your meringue thinly onto a parchment lined baking tray and place in the oven for around an hour. Check it after this time to see if it is hard and set. If not leave it in for another half hour until it has dried out but not coloured. Once cooked, turn your oven off, leave the door open an inch but leave your meringue in until needed.

FOR THE LAPSANG GEL:

While your pannacotta is setting and your meringue is cooking you can make the rest of the components.
The lapsang gel really brings this dish to life, by giving a smoky flavour that really helps the illusion. If you can get Twinings I strongly recommend it, but any other smoky lapsang will be fine.

Start off by putting your teabags in 380ml of just boiled water. Leave to steep for 5 minutes. Discard the teabags and bring to the boil. Whisk in the sugar and agar agar and boil for around 3 minutes, whisking constantly. Take off the heat and pour into a shallow tray. Leave in the fridge for around an hour to set.

Once set, break up the jelly into your smoothie blender and blitz for around a minute. It should blend to a smooth yet stable gel. If it's a bit lumpy or thick, add a tablespoon of water and blitz again until smooth. Transfer to your squeezy bottle of piping bag and chill until needed.

FOR THE CHOCOLATE CRUMB:

The chocolate crumb goes with the meringue ash to give the appearance of cigarette ash. Take your frozen chocolate and blitz in your smoothie blender or food processor. You want a small crumb, but not a fine powder. Pour your silver lustre powder into the smoothie cup with your crumb, replace the lid and shake until all the chocolate is coloured silver. Put aside until needed.

FOR THE CIGARETTE BUTTS:

Start off by melting your white chocolate. Take 1/3 and put to one side. Take the rest and add your orange food colouring gel drop by drop, stirring constantly. After a few drops the chocolate will start to thicken and turn into a paste. Keep doing this until you achieve a mouldable texture (a bit like play doh). If the colour gets too orange, you can use drops of cold water to help thicken instead.

Working quickly, use your hands to finish moulding the chocolate into a smooth texture (you may want to use gloves). You need to make 30 cylinder shapes around 1 inch long by 5mm thick (the size of cigarette butts). Cut each end to a flat finish and set aside. If youre feeling confident you can bend some to look like scrunched up butts.

Next take your remaining white chocolate and add half a teaspoon of water and mix. Add your icing sugar and stir until you get a paste the same thickness as before. Divide this into 30 pea sized balls, and flatten two sides to make small cylinders. Finally stick each one onto one end of each orange butt, roll on a flat surface till flush and put in the fridge to set.

When set, take your white chocolate bar and grate a fine dusting onto a flat surface. Roll each cigarette but once over the grated chocolate to create a slight spotty texture on each butt. Now it's time to bring the whole thing together...

TO ASSEMBLE:

Remove your pannacottas from the fridge. Squeeze an even layer of lapsang gel onto each, about 3mm thick. Next add small piles of silver chocolate crumb. Take your grey meringue and put into a food processor. Blitz to a fine dust and add small piles on your pannacotta. Carefully, use a spoon to mix the meringue dust and chocolate crumb topping so your ashtrays look messy and full of ash.

Finally add 5 chocolate butts to each ashtray, making sure to dip the white end into some meringue ash first.

GARNISHES

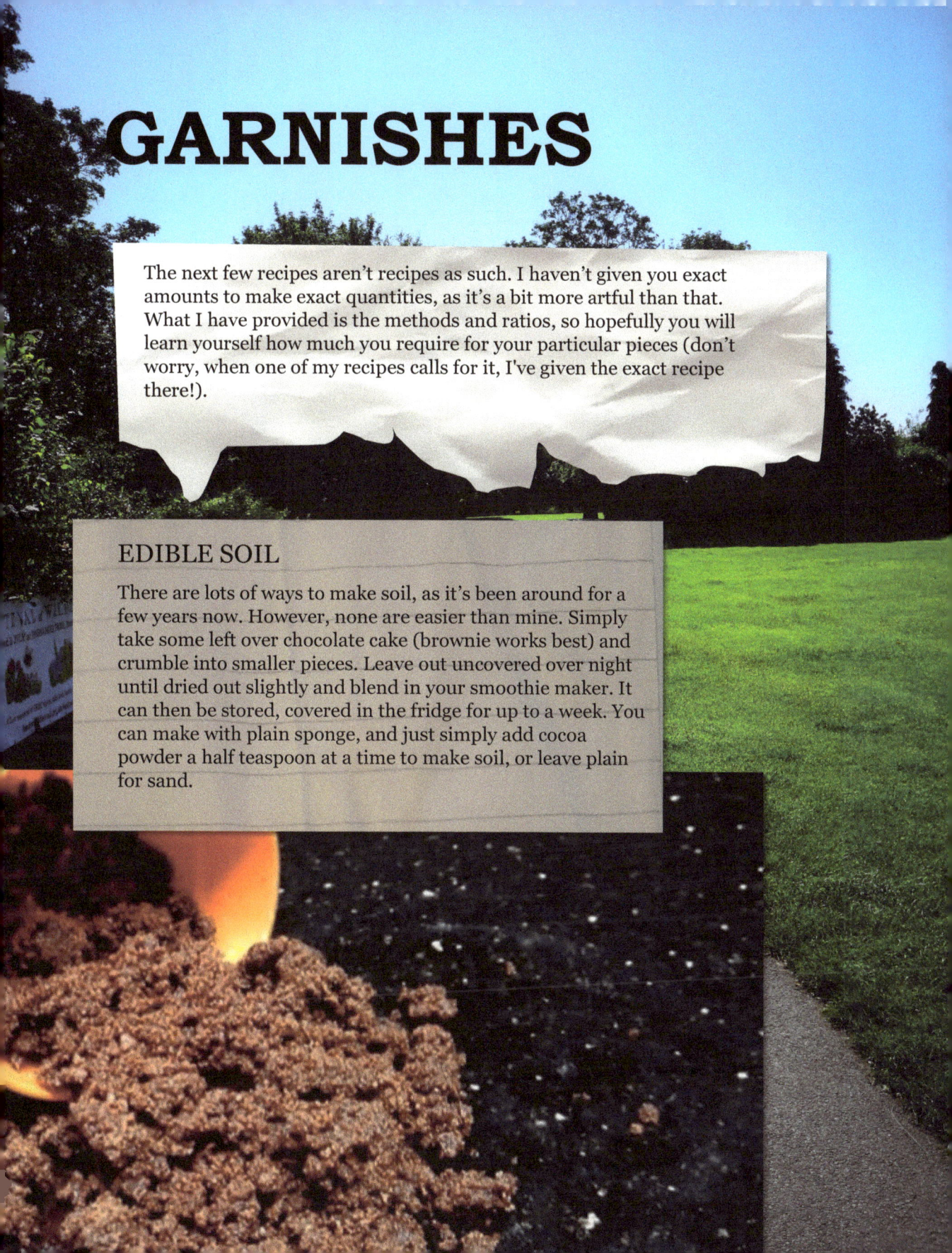

The next few recipes aren't recipes as such. I haven't given you exact amounts to make exact quantities, as it's a bit more artful than that. What I have provided is the methods and ratios, so hopefully you will learn yourself how much you require for your particular pieces (don't worry, when one of my recipes calls for it, I've given the exact recipe there!).

EDIBLE SOIL

There are lots of ways to make soil, as it's been around for a few years now. However, none are easier than mine. Simply take some left over chocolate cake (brownie works best) and crumble into smaller pieces. Leave out uncovered over night until dried out slightly and blend in your smoothie maker. It can then be stored, covered in the fridge for up to a week. You can make with plain sponge, and just simply add cocoa powder a half teaspoon at a time to make soil, or leave plain for sand.

TWIGS

Twigs are so easy but so effective. Melt some dark chocolate (be careful not to over heat) and put in a piping bag. Cut a 2mm hole in the end and simply pipe twig shapes onto a piece of baking parchment. Go as mad as you like but make sure they aren't too thin at the base end. Store in the fridge until needed.

BARK

Very similar in preparation to the twigs, start off by melting some dark chocolate. Take a piece of parchment and screw it up into the smallest ball you can. Unscrew, and spread your chocolate on. Leave to set in the fridge, but not perfectly flat. Once set, put the remaining chocolate into a piping bag and make a 1mm hole in the end. Unmould your bark from the parchment and drizzle chocolate onto the bumpy side. Leave to set for 5 minutes and brush lightly with cocoa powder.

HYBRID SAUCES: FROM SULTANA SYRUP TO APPLE PIE PUREE

You may notice a lack of sauces in this book, and there is a very good reason for this. I feel that saying a dish must go with a certain sauce is too restricting. All of the dishes in this book have recipes that have balanced flavours, textures and moistures. Just because it doesn't say "serve with pouring cream" doesn't mean you can't add a healthy glug at the end. The same goes for sauces. Personally, if I'm remaking a dish, 9 times out of 10 a component will change. Usually down to what's in season, what I have lying about, what's inspiring me at that time. I might make, for example, the dishwashing sponge. An olive oil sponge, with fresh mint, a rich toffee and deep baked apple flavours with the sharpness of granny smith, all topped off with sweet milk foam. This dish has been worked on and worked on by me to get the flavours and composition just how I want them, and what I feel is pleasing to the senses (which makes up for its appearance!). But you may make the dish, and decide to substitute the apple flavour for banana, taking it down a banoffee route. Brilliant! Go nuts, experiment, eat it however the hell you want! If you want to add some whipped cream, you add some cream. If you want to leave an element off, and if you feel it will make it better for you, do it. It's your dish, do what you want with it.

It's this thinking which has lead me to be so free with my food. "Why can't I make a chocolate and strawberry cake look like an iron throne?" This is what has led me to making sauces from everything and anything. I'll give you an example...

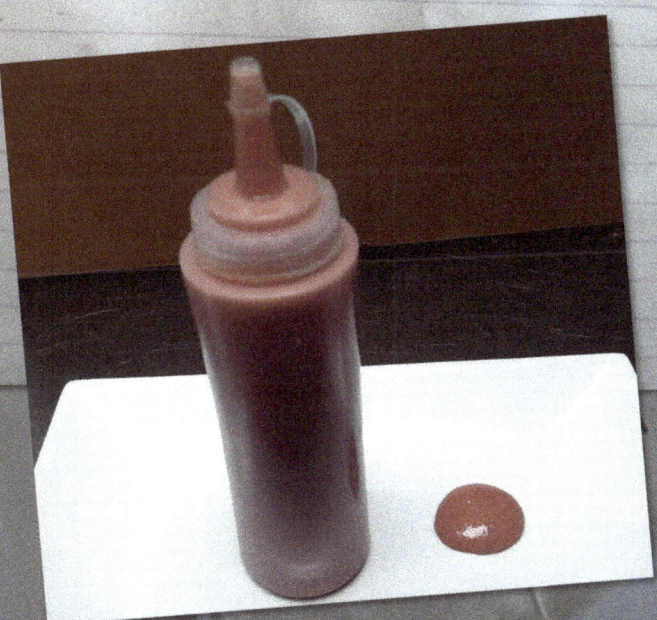

I was making my cold apple crumble; baked apple bavarois, granola, cold custard. Perfect on its own. There's depth, salt, sweetness, sharpness. But I had some apple pie kicking about. And I got thinking. How can I get that added flavour level of apple pie on the plate but with just one element? If I started to add too many new bits, it soon comes away from being a twist on an apple crumble and starts to become an apple tasting (which is fine by the way!). I was trying to figure out what makes the apple pie taste that you remember. The pastry? The custard? The stewed apple and cinnamon filling? Then it struck me! What if I blend a piece of apple pie with some custard? Would it lose its taste or retain it? So into the blender went a slice of pie, and some thin custard. What a eureka moment! Everything about pie in one simple sauce. So that went on the dish that time around. Another time in autumn, I had the sense of sultanas on my mind. I combined a simple sugar syrup with sultanas, left to steep, blended then strained. Perfect to drizzle around my apple.

I've not included these recipes, and many others, as I've only just started to explore the possibilities. Pear drop syrup, burnt water gel, orange soda curd, bubblegum coulis. All ideas that have worked on plates, all completely spontaneous, all brilliant. The only limit is your flavour profiling, your palate, and your imagination.

www.ingramcontent.com/pod-product-compliance
Lightning Source LLC
Chambersburg PA
CBHW041218240426
43661CB00012B/1081